# Football's
# Most Wanted
# II

**Also by Walter Harvey**

*The Super Bowl's Most Wanted: The Top 10 Book of Big-Game Heroes, Pigskin Zeroes, and Championship Oddities*

**Other football titles from Potomac Books, Inc.**

*The Pain Gang: Pro Football's Fifty Toughest Players*, Neil Reynolds

*Big Play: Barra on Football*, Allen Barra

*Coaching Matters: Leadership and Tactics of the NFL's Ten Greatest Coaches*, Brad Adler

*Dominance: The Best Seasons of Pro Football's Greatest Teams*, Eddie Epstein

*Playing Hurt: Evaluating and Treating the Warriors of the NFL*, Pierce E. Scranton

*Football's Most Wanted: The Top 10 Book of the Great Game's Outrageous Characters, Fortunate Fumbles, and Other Oddities*, Floyd Conner

# Football's Most Wanted II

## The Top 10 Book of More Bruising Backs, Savage Sacks, and Gridiron Oddities

Walter Harvey

Potomac Books, Inc.
Washington, D.C.

Library of Congress Cataloging-in-Publication Data
Harvey, Walter, 1967-
  Football's most wanted II : the top 10 book of more bruising backs, savage sacks, and gridiron oddities / by Walter Harvey.— 1st ed.
      p. cm.
  Includes bibliographical references and index.
  ISBN 1-57488-986-9 (pbk. : alk. paper)
  1. Football—Miscellanea. 2. Football players—Anecdotes. I. Title: Football's most wanted 2. II. Title: Football's most wanted two. III. Title.
  GV950.5H37 2006
  796.332—dc22

                                          2005028987


ISBN 1-57488-986-9

(alk. paper)

Printed in Canada on acid-free paper that meets the American National Standards Institute Z39-48 Standard.

Potomac Books, Inc.
22841 Quicksilver Drive
Dulles, Virginia 20166

First Edition

10  9  8  7  6  5  4  3  2  1

# Contents

# List of Photographs

# Acknowledgments

Special thanks go to Kevin Cuddihy, sports fan, editor extraordinaire, and really good guy. Without his guidance and suggestions, there would probably not be a *Football's Most Wanted II*. A shout out is also due to the entire team at Potomac Books. I only wrote it . . . they turned it into a book. Thanks also to Steve Herd, German Fragoso, Joe Bondi, Pete Woolley, Chris Roach, Bill Wingertzahn, and the immortal Chris Majkowski. Every morning on our email chains you leave me amused, enlightened, and at times befuddled. Plus you're the only group of people I know who can turn a discussion from Nikki Sixx to Thomas Pynchon in just six easy steps.

Lastly, thanks go to my beautiful wife, Larissa. When you're a Jets fan, like me, you never think good luck is on your side. But thanks to you, Larissa, I feel like I've won the Super Bowl every day. It would take pages to express how much you mean to me, so I'll just say this: when I was so messed up, and had opera in my head, your love was the light bulb hanging over my bed. Thanks for lighting my way.

# Introduction

The popularity of football in America continues to grow and grow. The Super Bowl is the most-watched television program every year, and networks are falling over themselves trying to get a piece of the NFL television package. On the college side, today we have the BCS, which at least makes an effort to crown a legitimate national champion, and we still have the ever-popular Heisman Trophy, although the winners of that award don't always experience professional success.

It's not just on the field where football is king. How about the NFL draft? Remember when you just read about who your team drafted in the paper the next day? Because it wasn't that long ago. And as we'll see here, being a high draft pick is no sure thing, and you can find some gems in the later rounds. Then there's the silver screen, where we've been treated to some classics like the original *The Longest Yard*. Okay, in the interest of fairness, yes, there have been some football movie clunkers, like you'll read here. Remember Gus the mule? No, well read on. Does being a football player help you score with beautiful women? Take a look at our list and judge for yourself.

If you're a man, I guarantee you'll have a little more respect for Bob Waterfield after you read this book.

You want to put the long hours in to become a football coach? Take a look at coaches who moved on from college to the pros, some successfully, and others with dismal results. And then we have guys like Pete Carroll, going back to school after coaching in the NFL. That's kind of worked out pretty well for him, huh?

But as always, the play is the thing. And in *Football's Most Wanted II,* you'll read about some of the great plays, wildest endings, super teams, lopsided rivalries, controversial calls, and unbelievable comebacks.

So without further ado, let's send it back for the second half kickoff!

# Boy, This Kid Looks Good!

When teams look ahead to a new season, one thing that is always a great unknown is how much their newcomers will contribute. Sometimes, despite the importance of veteran leadership, a first-year player makes a big difference. Here are ten of the best breakout rookie/freshman seasons.

## 1. HERSCHEL WALKER

1980 was a great year in Athens. Vince Dooley's Georgia Bulldogs won college football's national championship, thanks in large part to a quiet freshman running back by the name of Herschel Walker. A local product out of Wrightsville, Georgia, Walker exploded onto the scene, setting NCAA freshman records with 1,616 yards rushing, 200-yard rushing games (four), average rush yards per game (146.9), and rushing touchdowns (15). His best game was against Vanderbilt, when he rushed 23 times for 283 yards and three touchdowns. Walker would finish third in the Heisman voting, then cap off his stellar season with a touchdown in a Sugar Bowl win over Notre Dame.

## 2. JIM BROWN

The Cleveland Browns made one of the best draft selections of all time when they took Syracuse running back Jim Brown with their first pick in 1957. Brown lived up to all expectations by leading the league with 942 yards rushing (in a 12-game season) and nine touchdowns, which also led the league. In addition to making the Pro Bowl, Brown was named the Associated Press NFL Player of the Year and Offensive Rookie of the Year.

## 3. LAWRENCE TAYLOR

One year after Walker took the college world by storm, a rookie out of North Carolina came to the Big Apple and took over the NFL. The Giants had not been to the playoffs since 1963 (seven years before the merger), but LT signaled a change to the team's identity, and as a rookie guided the Giants not only to the playoffs, but to a win over defending NFC Champion Philadelphia in the Wild Card game. Taylor was a menace to quarterbacks from his outside linebacker position, and in 1981 launched his Hall of Fame career by earning honors as both the NFL Rookie of the Year and Defensive Player of the Year.

## 4. MARCUS DUPREE

Marcus Dupree came out of Mississippi to attend Oklahoma University and play running back for Barry Switzer's Sooners in 1982. A fabulous freshman season had Sooners fans thinking back to a recent phenom, Billy Sims. Despite injuries that limited his playing time, Dupree rushed for 905 yards as a freshman, then added 239 in a Fiesta Bowl loss to Arizona State. Dupree made the cover of *Sports Illustrated*, as much for his problems with head coach Switzer as for his on-field exploits. Because of an inability to coexist with his coach,

Dupree transferred to Southern Mississippi, later went to the USFL, but never became the star he looked like as a freshman at OU.

### 5. **MAURICE CLARETT**

Ohio State had not won a national championship in thirty-five seasons. But that changed when a dynamic running back came to Columbus in 2002. Maurice Clarett became an instant star for the Buckeyes, and he helped lead them to an unbeaten season and a national championship victory over Miami in the Fiesta Bowl. He finished with 1,190 yards, despite knee troubles that hampered him during the season, including a 230-yard game against Washington State and a 175-yard outing versus Texas Tech. He played just one year for the Buckeyes before becoming embroiled in scandal, but without Clarett, Ohio State might still be in the midst of their championship drought.

### 6. **ERIC DICKERSON**

Eric Dickerson left SMU in 1983 to have one of the best seasons for a rookie runner ever. An immediate starter as the number one draft pick of the Los Angeles Rams, Dickerson put up monster numbers: 1,808 yards rushing on 390 attempts (which both led the league). He scored 18 touchdowns on the ground, and on top of all that he also hauled in 51 receptions, leading the Rams to a wild card berth.

### 7. **RANDY MOSS**

Talent-wise, NFL scouts had Randy Moss tabbed as one of the top five players in the 1998 draft. But off-field issues dropped Moss late in the first round, where Dennis Green and the Vikings selected him. And quickly in his rookie year, he had opposing scouts in disbelief that they let him slip by in the draft. Moss caught 69 passes for 1,313 yards and a league-leading 17 touchdowns, despite constant double teams from defenses. His emergence was one of the primary reasons the Vikings were one of the most prolific offenses in history and put together a 15-win season.

### 8. ADRIAN PETERSON

Under head coach Bob Stoops, the Oklahoma Sooners have established themselves as one of the top programs in the country. And in 2004, the best player in Norman was a true freshman running back named Adrian Peterson. Peterson launched his career with a 100-yard performance on opening day versus Bowling Green, and he would rush for 100 or more in 11 of the Sooners' twelve regular season games, including 249 against rival Oklahoma State, and 225 in the Red River battle with Texas, both wins. For the season, in which he led the Sooners to the BCS Championship Game, Peterson rushed for 1,925 yards and 15 touchdowns.

### 9. MARSHALL FAULK

When Marshall Faulk left Louisiana to attend San Diego State in 1991, he found himself well down the running back depth chart before the season even started. But that changed quickly. In week 2, he was inserted into the game versus Pacific late in the first quarter, and proceeded to rush for an NCAA freshman record of 386 yards and seven touchdowns, and he became a household name. By week five, he had moved to first string (how did coach Al Lugenbill keep a guy who rushed for seven touchdowns in one game on the bench that long?), and would have an All-American type season, rushing for 1,429 yards and 21 touchdowns, and leading the Aztecs to their first bowl in five years.

JERRY LAIZURE

Oklahoma University's freshman phenom Adrian Peterson
in action.

## 10. BEN ROETHLISBERGER

The biggest team surprise in the NFL in 2004 was the Pittsburgh Steelers, who went from a franchise that didn't make the playoffs the previous year to a 15–1 juggernaut. And the biggest surprise on the Steelers was the play of their first-round draft pick, quarterback Ben Roethlisberger of Miami (Ohio). Replacing an injured Tommy Maddox in week 2, Roethlisberger took over as the starting quarterback, and led Pittsburgh to wins in each of his 13 starts. He passed for 2,621 yards and 17 touchdowns with only 11 interceptions, as the Steelers advanced to the AFC Championship Game.

# Who Is This Guy?

NFL rosters have been the home of a number of famous American names—but they're not who you think they may be.

### 1. MICHAEL JACKSON
The King of Pop never ran a route across the middle on third down, as far as we know. But in an eight-year career with the Browns and Ravens, Michael Jackson was a favorite target of both Bernie Kosar and Vinnie Testaverde. His 1996 season was a thriller when he hauled in seventy-six passes for 1,201 yards and fourteen touchdowns to earn a Pro Bowl bid.

### 2. TONY BENNETT
In 1990 the Green Bay Packers spent their first-round draft pick on a linebacker out of Alabama, Tony Bennett. It must have been great to hear him croon his college fight song on training camp hazing day. Bennett spent four years with Green Bay and another four with the Colts. In an odd coincidence, while Bennett roamed the field for the Packers, across town

the top player on the Wisconsin–Green Bay NCAA tournament basketball squad was a sharpshooting guard named— you guessed it—Tony Bennett.

### 3. SAM ADAMS

The only connection Sam Adams, a mammoth defensive tackle out of Texas A&M, has with American patriot Samuel Adams is that he looks like he's had one or two of the beers named after Boston's hero. For four teams over eleven seasons, Adams has played an important role as a space-eater and disrupter on the defensive line, and he helped the Baltimore Ravens to a Super Bowl championship following the 2000 season.

### 4. NEILL ARMSTRONG

Armstrong played five seasons as a wide receiver for the Eagles from 1947 through 1951, but he is best remembered (if at all) for his four-season stint as head coach of the Chicago Bears. In 1979, during his second year, the Bears took one small step into the playoffs as a wild card, but they never made that giant leap to the Super Bowl under Armstrong, who finished his career with a 30–34 won-loss record.

### 5. CHARLIE BROWN

Good grief! There were, in fact, three Charlie Browns to play in the NFL. The most famous played six years with the Redskins and Falcons, and his best year was in 1983 for Washington, when he caught seventy-eight passes for more than 1,200 yards and eight touchdowns. The previous year he caught a Super Bowl–clinching touchdown pass from Joe Theismann in the Redskins' win over the Dolphins. And he never had a ball pulled out from under him while attempting a field goal!

## 6. **BILL BRADLEY**

Senator Bill Bradley is widely remembered as one of the key contributors to two New York Knicks NBA championships. Another Bill Bradley was a widely respected defensive back for the Eagles from 1969 through 1976. He was named All-Pro three times and still shares (with Eric Allen) the Philadelphia career record of thirty-four interceptions. For the past two decades he's been coaching in the CFL, USFL, and NFL, and he is currently the defensive coordinator on Guy Morriss's staff at Baylor University. Just don't expect him to run for president any time soon.

## 7. **EDDIE MURRAY**

No, he's not a Hall of Fame first baseman, but Eddie Murray was one of the NFL's premier placekickers in a career that spanned two decades. He scored more than 100 points six times, including in 1993, the year he won his only Super Bowl ring as a member of the Dallas Cowboys.

## 8. **HENRY FORD**

This defensive tackle motored onto the scene from the University of Arkansas to the Houston Oilers in 1994. His best season in a ten-year career came in the Titans' 1999 AFC Championship season, when he recorded 5.5 sacks.

## 9. **STEVE MARTIN**

The wild and crazy journeyman defensive tackle out of Ole Miss has taken a lot of planes, trains, and automobiles throughout his career. In nine seasons Martin has played for seven teams, making stops in Indianapolis, Philadelphia, Kansas City, New York (as a Jet), New England, Houston, and Minnesota.

## 10. DARRYL HALL

A defensive back out of Washington, Hall played three years in Canada for the Calgary Stampeders, then moved south. He lasted only three years in the NFL with the Broncos and 49ers, intercepting just one pass and proving that he wasn't very good playing "one on one" defense. But Hall was not deterred, and he returned to the Stampeders, for whom he played another five seasons and returned two interceptions for touchdowns.

# Football by the Numbers

Baseball is the sport that most fans associate with individual performance numbers, but as the following list shows, football is a game of numbers as well; some good, some not so good.

### 1. FOUR
In a 1998 first-round playoff game against the Green Bay Packers, 49ers wide receiver Terrell Owens dropped four passes, and the boo-birds at Candlestick were getting louder with each drop. Despite Owens's case of the dropsies, Steve Young called his number for the most important play of the game. With eight ticks remaining, Young fired over the middle towards Owens and the goal line. Even surrounded by Packers' defenders, he hauled in the touchdown, giving the 49ers a 30–27 win.

### 2. TWENTY-EIGHT
In 1976 the two-time defending Super Bowl champion Steelers were reeling with a 1–4 record, and the Steel Curtain had clearly had enough. Over the final nine games, the Steelers went 9–0, but their defense allowed just twenty-eight points,

including five shutouts (and sixteen of those twenty-eight came in one game, against the Bengals).

### 3. NINETEEN
As a freshman at Marshall University in 1996, wide receiver Randy Moss staked claim to being one of the best players in the country. Moss caught nineteen touchdown passes that year, an NCAA Division IAA record for freshmen.

### 4. TWO
How close were the 1983 Washington Redskins to a perfect regular season? How about two points? The Redskins lost only two games all year: a 31–30 loss to the Cowboys on the Monday Night opener, in which they blew a big halftime lead; and a 48–47 heartbreaker to the Packers, when Mark Moseley missed a potential game-winning field goal at the gun.

### 5. TWO
In the 1942 Sugar Bowl Fordham proved that you don't need to put up a lot of points to win a football game. The Rams recorded just two points on a safety, but that was enough to knock off the Missouri Tigers.

### 6. EIGHT
In nine NFL seasons the great Jim Brown led the league in rushing eight times (the only other man to win the rushing title while Brown was active was Green Bay's Jim Taylor). Eight times might not seem all that impressive, but is more so when you realize that the next closest men won four in a row, including this impressive foursome: O.J. Simpson, Eric Dickerson, Emmitt Smith, and Barry Sanders.

### 7. **FIFTY-EIGHT**

Elsewhere in this book you can read the story of Doug Flutie's Hail Mary to beat the Miami Hurricanes at the Orange Bowl in 1984. The following season, the Hurricanes began a home winning streak that would last almost a full decade. Miami took fifty-eight consecutive games at the Orange Bowl—a streak that lasted until 1994, when Ray Lewis, Warren Sapp, and company could not stop the University of Washington from toppling the Hurricanes 38–20.

### 8. **SEVENTY-SIX**

Think David Carr was sore after the Houston Texans' inaugural 2002 season? Carr suffered through a year in which he was sacked seventy-six times, breaking an NFL record that was set in 1986, when Randall Cunningham was dropped seventy-two times for the Eagles.

### 9. **NINETEEN**

Kevin Miller of East Carolina set a Bowl game record for points by a kicker during the 2001 GMAC Bowl against Marshall. In a wild game that went into two overtimes, Miller notched seven PATs and four field goals for nineteen total points.

### 10. **TWELVE**

In the 1970s a lot of kids throughout the country were wearing football jerseys with the number 12 on them. Why number 12? Twelve of the first fourteen Super Bowl champions had a quarterback wearing that number, including Bart Starr, Joe Namath, Roger Staubach, Bob Griese, Ken Stabler, and Terry Bradshaw. The two teams led to a title by non-number 12s? Kansas City in Super Bowl IV, quarterbacked by number 16 Len Dawson, and Baltimore, who won Super Bowl V with number 15 Earl Morrall.

# It's War Out There

Football is just a game. So why is it often described using terms from a military engagement? Here are some battlefield terms often associated with football.

### 1. SACK
When invading armies overran towns then stripped them of their goods, they were said to have sacked the town. In football, Deacon Jones coined the term "sack" to describe defensive players trying to overrun the offensive line in order to tackle the quarterback.

### 2. BLITZ
Military units blitz their enemy by using overwhelming force with lightning quick speed to take out a target, sometimes with both air and ground force. In football, defenses try to "blitz" offenses by sending a large number of players to infiltrate the backfield and disrupt or sack the quarterback.

### 3. BATTLE
Gettysburg was a battle. Antietam was a battle. Normandy was a battle. Football games are not battles. However, especially close games are often referred to that way. There are

individual "battles" as well, as in, "Eddie George and Ray Lewis have some battle going on out there."

### 4. BOMB

Perhaps the most-used military analogy in football is the bomb. Any long pass from a quarterback to a receiver is called a "bomb," and it's appropriate, as a long pass drops out of the sky just like a real bomb.

### 5. FIELD GENERAL

Quarterbacks who have a habit of successfully moving the ball down the field, like Brett Favre, are sometimes referred to as field generals. Of course, historic field generals like Rommel and Patton must turn over in their graves any time they hear this.

### 6. WAR ROOM

Before entering into battle, leaders map out their strategies in war rooms. On draft day in the NFL, with teams resorting to large charts, spread sheets, and computer graphics, some have taken to referring to teams' draft rooms as "war rooms."

### 7. AERIAL ATTACK

The might of an air force can be indispensable in times of war—witness the fierce American air assaults during the two Gulf wars. "Aerial attacks" help soften things up for ground forces. In football, it's the other way around: a good rushing game opens things up for the aerial attack, or passing game.

### 8. IN THE TRENCHES

There may be no more frightening place in the world than the trenches during a ground battle. Chaos reigns amidst gunfire, shouting, and bomb blasts. In football, "in the trenches" refers to the scrums along the line of scrimmage. Usually the team that wins "in the trenches" is the team that emerges triumphantly.

## 9. SPY

Information. It's one of the most important facets of war—getting knowledge into the hands of the uniformed men before they step into battle. The "spy" in football is fairly new. With the proliferation of younger, quicker quarterbacks like Michael Vick, defenses have taken to using a "spy," usually a linebacker, whose job it is to contain the quarterback and prevent him from taking off on a long run.

## 10. SLAUGHTER

When an attack is terribly vicious and overpowering, and when the invading army is unable to be stopped, that is an onslaught. Tremendous offensive attacks occur in football when an offense jumps on an opposing team and never lets up. Remember Super Bowl XXIV? San Francisco jumped all over Denver and beat them 55–10, in a textbook football "onslaught."

# Close To Perfect

Ever since 1972, when the Miami Dolphins finished off a perfect 17–0 season with a 14–7 win over the Washington Redskins in Super Bowl VII, veterans from that team have gathered for a champagne toast whenever a final unbeaten squad goes down. Here are some of the teams that have come closest to matching the Dolphins.

### 1. 1985 CHICAGO BEARS
The 1985 Bears had a couple of early season struggles: a surprisingly tough win over Tampa Bay in week one at Soldier Field, and a dramatic come-from-behind win over Minnesota a few games later. From there they rolled to a 12–0 record and had a week thirteen matchup with Miami, of all teams. In the Orange Bowl. On Monday night. With members of the 1972 Dolphins team on the sidelines. Bears quarterback Jim McMahon was hurt, and missed the game, and Miami, led by Dan Marino, jumped out to a big lead and coasted to a 38–24 win. It was the only defeat for the Bears, who that season finished 15–1 and won Super Bowl XX.

### 2. 1998 DENVER BRONCOS
The 1985 Bears are the team best remembered for their run

at perfection, but one team that actually came closer to the Dolphins was the 1998 Denver Broncos. The defending Super Bowl champions were 13–0 facing a two-game road trip: First at the Meadowlands against the lowly Giants; then—you guessed it, at Miami on a Monday night. It looked for sure like the events of 1985 might play out again, but the Giants threw a wrench in the plans. The Broncos blew a fourth quarter lead and New York's Kent Graham engineered the winning drive to spring the upset. Denver lost the following week to the Dolphins but finished 14–2 and won their second consecutive Super Bowl.

### 3. 1984 SAN FRANCISCO 49ERS

They were not as flashy as the 1985 Bears, but the 49ers were darn close to perfect one year earlier. The Niners lost but one game, a 20–17 defeat at the hands of the Pittsburgh Steelers in week seven at Candlestick Park. They and the Bears are the only teams to win fifteen regular season games and win the Super Bowl.

### 4. 1998 MINNESOTA VIKINGS

The 1998 Vikings set a record by scoring 556 points, an average of more than thirty-four per game, on their way to a 15–1 record. The only blemish was a 27–24 loss to the Buccaneers in Tampa Bay in week eight. The Vikings' path to the Super Bowl was stopped in the NFC Championship Game, where they lost in overtime to the Atlanta Falcons.

### 5. 2004 PITTSBURGH STEELERS

The Steelers did not threaten the 1972 Dolphins for long—they lost in week two to the Ravens—but the two teams do share something in common: They're the only two teams to win fourteen consecutive games in the same season. After a

1–1 start, the Steelers did not lose again until a 41–27 loss to the New England Patriots in the AFC Championship Game.

## 6. 1990 SAN FRANCISCO 49ERS

In 1990 the 49ers looked like they were positioned to be the first team to win three straight Super Bowls. They coasted through their first ten games, with two games against NFC heavyweights coming up on their schedule: the Los Angeles Rams, who the Niners had defeated in the previous year's NFC Championship Game; and the 10–0 New York Giants (more on them below). But the battle of the unbeatens never materialized as the Rams upset the 49ers 28–17. San Francisco eventually faltered on their way to a three-peat, dropping the NFC Championship Game at home to the Giants.

## 7. 1990 NEW YORK GIANTS

As mentioned above, the Giants also sported a 10–0 mark in 1990, but their regular season took a downturn from that point, with losses to the Eagles, the 49ers, and the Bills (all playoff teams) in their final six games. They finished 13–3; but New York regrouped in the postseason to upset two of those teams (San Francisco and Buffalo) on their way to winning Super Bowl XXV.

## 8. 2003–2004 NEW ENGLAND PATRIOTS

The Patriots broke the all-time regular season record for consecutive wins by taking the final twelve games of the 2003 season and the first six of 2004 to win eighteen straight, something even the great Dolphins could not claim. The Dolphins won sixteen in a row over three seasons: the final game of 1971, all fourteen of 1972, and game one of 1973. The previous record of seventeen consecutive wins was held by the 1933–34 Chicago Bears.

### 9. 1977 DALLAS COWBOYS

The Cowboys started 1977 with eight straight wins and appeared to have only one real test remaining on their schedule: a week ten trip to Pittsburgh to take on the Steelers. But in week nine, Dallas may have been caught looking ahead. On a Monday night in Texas Stadium, the St. Louis Cardinals upset the Cowboys 24–17. Dallas lost again the following week in Pittsburgh, but those would be their only losses of the season. They finished 12–2 and won Super Bowl XII.

### 10. 2005 INDIANAPOLIS COLTS

Peyton Manning and the Colts made a run at perfection that lasted well into December. A 26–18 win over the Jaguars in Jacksonville gave Indianapolis a 13–0 record, and they needed to win just three more games to finish the regular season undefeated. But one week later, the San Diego Chargers stormed into the RCA Dome and dropped a 26–17 loss on the Colts. The Colts, with their division title already wrapped up, rested their regulars the following week when they lost to the eventual NFC Champion Seahawks in Seattle, and in their season finale win over the Cardinals. With a 14–2 record, the Colts had home field advantage throughout the AFC playoffs but were upset 21–18 in the divisional playoffs by the Steelers, who would go on to win the Super Bowl.

# Aren't You A Little Old For This?

Every coach loves a player with experience. Well, how about a player with a couple of decades' experience? Through the 2004 season, forty-three men had played in the NFL at age forty or older. Following is a list of ten of those veterans.

## 1. GEORGE BLANDA

When quarterback/placekicker George Blanda retired at the end of the 1975 season following twenty-six years in the league, he was 48, the oldest player to ever suit up in an NFL game—*and* he held the record for career points. How remarkable was Blanda's longevity? When he started in 1949, the Korean War had yet to start, Harry Truman was in the White House, and many of his teammates had yet to be born. When he said goodbye to the game, Ford was President, Saigon had just fallen, and he was nine years older than his head coach, John Madden.

## 2. GARY ANDERSON

Through 2004, when Anderson, a placekicker, played for the Tennessee Titans at the age of 45, he had compiled a record for career points with 2,434 over twenty-three years. The high-light came in 1998 with a perfect regular season (not a single miss on a field goal or PAT) for the 15–1 Minnesota Vikings.

### 3. MORTEN ANDERSEN

Like Gary Anderson, Morten Andersen came into the league in 1982, and by 2004 he was still kicking—literally and figu-ratively. The 44-year-old Andersen finished the 2004 season with the Vikings second on the all-time scoring list with 2,358 points, second only to Gary Anderson.

### 4. STEVE DeBERG

A teammate of Morten Andersen with the Falcons in 1998, DeBerg came out of a four-year retirement to back up quar-terback Chris Chandler for Dan Reeves's team. During his hiatus from playing, DeBerg served as an assistant coach under Reeves, but he was back as an active player at age 44. He played in nine games, with a couple of starts for the 14–2 NFC champion Falcons.

### 5. WARREN MOON

Like DeBerg, Warren Moon was still calling signals at age 44. The seventeen-year NFL veteran, who began his professional career in the CFL, saw limited action for Gunther Cunningham's Kansas City Chiefs in 2000, completing just fifteen of thirty-four passes, with one touchdown and one interception.

### 6. EDDIE MURRAY

Best known for his long, stellar career with the Detroit Lions, Eddie Murray retired in 2000 at the age of 44. A twenty-one-year veteran, he played out his final games with Norv Turner's Washington Redskins. In 1993 Murray won his lone Super Bowl ring as kicker for Jimmy Johnson's Dallas Cowboys.

### 7. **LOU GROZA**

"The Toe" finished up his twenty-one-year career with the Cleveland Browns in 1967 at the age of 43. The Hall of Fame offensive tackle and kicker (hence, the nickname) spent his final seven seasons exclusively kicking. He retired with 1,608 points, the most ever at the time.

### 8. **JAN STENERUD**

In nineteen seasons, Stenerud never missed a game due to injury and finished his Hall of Fame career with the Vikings in 1985 at the age of 43. He went to six Pro Bowls, helped the Chiefs win Super Bowl IV, and is the only pure placekicker enshrined in Canton.

### 9. **JERRY RICE**

To all the achievements Jerry Rice has earned in his twenty-year career (he's the all-time leader in receptions, receiving yards, receiving touchdowns, and yards from scrimmage), add one more: oldest wide receiver in NFL history. He finished his career in 2004 (which he split between Oakland and Seattle) with thirty receptions for 429 yards and two touchdowns at the age of 42. No other wide receiver has played into his forties.

### 10. **DOUG FLUTIE**

As a backup to Drew Brees, the 42-year-old Flutie played two games for the AFC West champion San Diego Chargers in 2004. He completed twenty of thirty-eight passes with one touchdown and also rushed five times (a Flutie specialty, even in his forties) for thirty-nine yards and a couple of touchdowns. In the final game of the 2005 season as a member of the Patriots, he converted the first dropkick extra point in the NFL since 1941, when he scored against the Miami Dolphins.

# Aren't You A Little Young For This?

When you think of NFL coaches, you get an image of a gruff, graying, older man with a pained look on his face, barking out orders. The following guys not only did not fit that mold, but they all had players who were older than them. Here are the ten youngest head coaches in NFL history.

### 1. HARLAND SVARE

At 31 years, 11 months, Svare became the youngest head coach in league history when he took over the Los Angeles Rams after Bob Waterfield resigned during the 1962 season. In Svare's case, youth didn't make up for inexperience, as he put together just a 14–31–3 record in three-plus seasons with the Rams. In 1971 he got another chance at age 40, taking over for Sid Gilman in San Diego. He lasted just two years with the Chargers, going 7–17–2.

### 2. JOHN MICHELOSEN

In 1948 the Steelers named the 32-year-old Michelosen as their head coach, and he was the youngest NFL coach until Svare came along. But like most coaches during the early decades of football in the Steel City, Michelosen had little success. His four-year record wasn't awful (20–26–2), but it was enough to get him dismissed from what would be his only NFL head coaching job.

### 3. **DAVID SHULA**

The best thing you can say about David Shula's coaching is . . . um, oh, yeah, his last name is Shula. The son of Hall of Fame coach Don Shula, David Shula took over the Bengals in 1991 at the age of 32, replacing Sam Wyche. Under Wyche, the Bengals were perennial contenders in the AFC Central, even reaching the Super Bowl in 1988. But Cincinnati never even had a whiff of the playoffs under Shula. They went 19–52 in his four-plus seasons. His final game with the Bengals marked the end of his NFL head coaching career.

### 4. **JOHN MADDEN**

Before he became a television and video game phenomenon, John Madden was the wildly successful head coach of the Oakland Raiders for a decade. It all started when Al Davis named the 32-year-old Madden to replace John Rauch after the 1968 season. Rauch had problems with Davis, so he moved on to become coach of the Bills after leading the Raiders to the Super Bowl. Madden went on to win 103 games in ten seasons—with eight playoff berths and a Super Bowl title, before he retired to the broadcast booth.

### 5. **DON SHULA**

About the only place you'll find David Shula listed ahead of his father is here. David was five months younger than his dad when each got their first jobs. Don turned 33 just a few days before he was named head coach of the Baltimore Colts in 1964, the first chapter in a storybook career. In thirty-three years with Baltimore and Miami, Shula set an NFL record with

328 wins and took his teams to six Super Bowls (plus the 1964 NFL Championship Game) winning two. In 1972 his Dolphins set the gold standard for NFL teams by going undefeated and winning Super Bowl VII.

## 6. AL DAVIS

Yes, before he stepped up to the front office to become a thorn in the side of AFL and NFL executives alike, 33-year-old Al Davis, a one-time assistant with the Chargers, became Raiders head coach in 1963. He led the Silver and Black for three years, going 23–16–3 over that stretch, before giving way to John Rauch in 1966.

## 7. JOE COLLIER

Joe Collier was 33 when he guided the Buffalo Bills to the playoffs in 1966—his first season with the team—but things fell apart soon after. Early in his third season, Collier was dismissed with an overall mark of 13–16–1.

## 8. BOB SNYDER

In 1948 the Rams named 33-year-old Snyder as their coach. It was his only NFL job, and he only held it for one year, in which his team went 6–6.

## 9. JOE TRIMBLE

The 34-year-old Trimble became head coach of the Eagles in 1952. In four years he kept his teams in contention (they finished second each year), but he never got them over the top. His final record in Philadelphia was 25–20–3.

## 10. JON GRUDEN

The third Raiders coach on this list, "Chucky," as Gruden is known for his resemblance to the doll in the *Child's Play* movies, was 34 when he took over the reins in Oakland in 1998. Gruden's first seven years as a head coach (with both Oakland and Tampa Bay) included a relatively modest 62–50 overall record, but he boasted three playoff appearances and a Super Bowl win with the Buccaneers. In that game Gruden became the youngest coach to win a Super Bowl and the second (following Weeb Ewbank) to beat his previous team (Oakland) in the game.

# Great Careers After Moving Teams

When you think of Hall of Famers and other great players, you tend to remember them in the uniforms they made famous (like Lawrence Taylor with the Giants or Dick Butkus with the Bears). But some greats began their careers with different teams, who gave up on them. Here are ten such players.

### 1. JOHNNY UNITAS
He's widely regarded as the best quarterback of all time, but the Pittsburgh Steelers apparently did not think too highly of him. Unitas was drafted by the Steelers—his hometown team—in the ninth round of the 1955 draft, but he never played a down with them. He was signed by the Colts before the following season, and by his third year in Baltimore he brought them a championship. In a Colts career that would last through 1972, Johnny U. threw for more than 40,000 yards and 290 touchdowns. He won three world championships and once set an NFL record with touchdown completions in forty-seven consecutive games.

## 2. BRETT FAVRE

Early in the second round of the 1991 draft the Atlanta Falcons selected strong-armed quarterback Brett Favre out of Southern Mississippi—much to the chagrin of the New York Jets, who had the next pick. The Jets, who were without a first-round selection, needed a quarterback and had listed Favre as the number one player on their draft board. Favre spent his rookie year backing up the immortal Chris Miller and Billy Joe Tolliver in Atlanta. Following the season, he was traded to Green Bay, whose new general manager, Ron Wolf, was the man running the Jets draft a year earlier and had coveted Favre. After replacing Don Majkowski early in the 1992 season, Favre started 221 consecutive games, won three MVP awards and a Super Bowl ring, and, until 2005, never had a losing season.

## 3. MARSHALL FAULK

Marshall Faulk was a very good player for the Indianapolis Colts in his first five years, which included four 1,000-yard rushing seasons. But in 1999 he was shipped to the Rams, where he had three years that were simply off the charts. From 1999 through 2001, he recorded 6,767 total yards from scrimmage, fifty-nine touchdowns, and averaged more than eighty catches out of the backfield. He also led the Rams, a team that had missed the postseason for a decade, to three straight playoff appearances, two NFC championships, and one Super Bowl title.

## 4. FRAN TARKENTON

Tarkenton actually had good years after moving *twice*. After six years in Minnesota, he was traded to the New York Giants, where he played for five seasons. Then he was sent back to Minnesota, where he played out his last seven years, leading the Vikings to three Super Bowl appearances along the way.

### 5. LEN DAWSON

Len Dawson was given up on by two NFL teams before he launched a Hall of Fame career with the Dallas Texans/Kansas City Chiefs of the AFL. (The Texans became the Chiefs when the franchise moved cities.) Dawson spent three years in Pittsburgh (1957–59) and saw little playing time; the same was true of two years in Cleveland (Let's take a moment to point out that in the mid- to late 1950s, the Steelers had both Johnny Unitas and Len Dawson and never gave either one a shot). Hank Stram, the Texans' coach, remembered Dawson from his college days and gave him an opportunity. He ended up playing fourteen years with the Texans/Chiefs, and he helped the Chiefs win Super Bowl IV, no doubt with the extra motivation of beating the league that had spurned him.

### 6. DON MAYNARD

The fleet Texan played for the New York Giants in 1958, then after one year of disillusionment with the NFL, hooked up with the CFL. Two years later he became the first signee of the AFL's New York Titans (later Jets). He quickly established himself as a star, then became a favorite target of Joe Namath, finishing his career with 11,834 yards receiving and eighty-eight touchdowns. Much like Dawson, he felt snubbed by the NFL early in his career, which gave him extra motivation when the Jets beat the NFL champion Colts in Super Bowl III.

### 7. PAUL KRAUSE

From 1964 through 1967 safety Paul Krause patrolled the secondary of the Washington Redskins, including a twelve-interception season as a rookie. Traded to the Vikings before the 1968 season, Krause played twelve of his Hall of Fame years in Minnesota. He started four Super Bowls and set the all-time record for career interceptions with eighty-one.

## 8. JOHN RIGGINS

Riggins played five years with the New York Jets, setting a team record with 1,005 yards rushing in 1975. But disagreements with management and questions about his relationship with Joe Namath prompted a trade to Washington. In nine years with the Redskins he rushed for more than 1,000 yards four times, and he rushed for more than 100 yards in six postseason games, including his MVP performance in Super Bowl XVII.

## 9. DARYL LAMONICA

The "Mad Bomber," best known for leading the Oakland Raiders to Super Bowl II, spent four years in Buffalo backing up Jack Kemp before being traded to Oakland. He led the Raiders on a remarkable three-year regular season stretch from 1967–69, when they went 37–4–1.

## 10. CORNELIUS BENNETT

Bennett was drafted by the Colts out of Alabama in 1987, but he never played a down for them. He was traded to Buffalo as part of a three-team deal that brought Eric Dickerson to Indianapolis. Bennett became one of the defensive stalwarts of a Bills team that went to four straight Super Bowls.

# Snow Blind

Is there any better kind of football game to watch than one being played in a snowstorm? It's just great to see players slip and slide through the white stuff, and there have been many memorable games played in the snow over the years. Here are some of the classics.

### 1. NEW ENGLAND VERSUS OAKLAND

The final game ever played at Foxboro Stadium pitted the Patriots and Raiders in a January 2002 divisional playoff game in heavy snow. Nursing a 13–10 lead late in the fourth quarter, the Raiders appeared to have clinched the game when Charles Woodson sacked Patriots quarterback Tom Brady, forcing a fumble recovered by the Raiders. But the ball was ruled an incomplete pass—infuriating the Raiders—in a decision that will forever be remembered as "The Tuck Rule." The Pats tied the game moments later on a remarkable 45-yard field goal through the snow by Adam Vinatieri. Vinatieri later won the game in overtime on a 23-yard field goal, a victory that propelled the Pats to their first Super Bowl championship.

### 2. NEW ENGLAND VERSUS MIAMI

Before the Tuck game, there was another famous snow game

played in Foxboro. Back in December of 1982 the Patriots hosted the Dolphins. Thanks to a steady snow the game stayed scoreless for the first three quarters. With a little less than five minutes left, New England drove inside the Dolphins 20-yard line. Facing fourth down, New England kicker John Smith trotted out onto the field to attempt a 23-yard field goal. But coach Ron Meyer had a trick up his sleeve. He called for a guy riding a manned snowplow to come off the sideline and clear a path for Smith. Smith's kick was good and the Patriots had a 3–0 victory. After the game it was revealed that the man driving the snowplow was on leave from prison on a work-release program.

### 3. CHICAGO VERSUS GREEN BAY

In 1932 the Bears played their home games at Wrigley Field, and their December home game against the Packers was played in a snowstorm that dropped six inches onto the field. Five thousand brave (or a little crazy) souls gathered at Wrigley to see the home team break a scoreless tie in the fourth quarter. Following a field goal, Hall of Famer Bronko Nagurski scored the game's only touchdown on a 56-yard run for a 9–0 Bears win.

### 4. MISSISSIPPI STATE VERSUS TEXAS A&M

A college bowl game played in a driving snowstorm? In Shreveport. In one of the more memorable bowl games in recent memory, Mississippi State and Texas A&M hooked up in the 2000 Independence Bowl. The snowstorm was close to blinding, but that didn't stop either offense. Mississippi State back Donte Walker had 143 yards rushing and three touchdowns, while A&M running back JaMar Toombs ran thirty-five times for 193 yards. He also scored three touchdowns as regulation ended with the score tied at 35. A Toombs touchdown gave A&M the lead, but the PAT was blocked and returned through the snow for a rare defensive 2-point conversion. With the score 41–37, Mississippi State quarterback Wayne Madkin scored the decisive points with a 6-yard touchdown run. The Bulldogs won 43–41.

### 5. PHILADELPHIA VERSUS CHICAGO CARDINALS

The 1948 NFL Championship Game fell on the same day as one of the Northeast's worst blizzards. Still, more than thirty-six thousand fans filled Shibe Park in Philadelphia to watch the Chicago Cardinals and the Eagles. The snow was so bad that fans came out of the stands to help players clear the field. Imagine players—even fans—doing that today. Steve Van Buren's 5-yard touchdown run early in the fourth quarter proved to be the game's only score in a 7–0 win, as the Eagles avenged a loss to the Cardinals in the previous season's championship game.

### 6. DENVER VERSUS GREEN BAY

The Broncos and Packers met in one of the most memorable Super Bowls, following the 1997 season. But a more memorable game between the two teams was thirteen years earlier, on an October Monday night in Mile High Stadium. A driving storm dropped six inches of snow on the field, and the Broncos dropped the hammer on the Packers in the first minute of the game. Denver became the first team in history to score twice without taking a snap. On Green Bay's first play, safety Steve Foley scooped up a fumble and raced in for a touchdown. On the very next play, Louis Wright gathered up another fumble and scored. Before you could blink, the score was 14–0. Green Bay mounted a furious comeback, as Lynn Dickey threw for 371 yards, more than 200 of those going to James Lofton. But it wasn't enough, and the Broncos held on for a 17–14 win.

## 7. **MICHIGAN VERSUS OHIO STATE**

The bitterest of rivals faced off in the bitterest of elements in this 1950 clash. With temperatures in the low teens and steady snow, this game would come to be known as the "Snow Bowl." The two teams combined for just 68 yards total offense and three first downs (all by Ohio State). They also combined for forty-five (!) punts, twenty-four of them by Michigan. The Wolverines were able to overcome the elements, thanks to two blocked punts: one that went through the end zone for a safety; and the other, which they recovered for a touchdown. Those were Michigan's only points in their 9–3 win. The victory sent the Wolverines to the Rose Bowl.

## 8. **GREEN BAY VERSUS TAMPA BAY**

The Packers welcomed their rivals from Florida to an old-fashioned Lambeau Field football game in December 1985. In snow so bad that fans were urged to stay home, Lynn Dickey put on a passing clinic, leading Green Bay to a 21–0 win. Despite the blizzard, more than nineteen thousand fans made it to the game, a pretty good showing even if it was their smallest crowd in thirty-three seasons.

## 9. **COLGATE VERSUS WESTERN ILLINOIS**

In 2003 the Colgate Raiders had a magical season, finishing the regular season undefeated and earning a number 4 seed in the Division 1AA football playoffs. With the high seed came home field advantage in their first two games, and after they beat UMass in the snow in the first round, Western Illinois made the trip to Hamilton, New York. A foot of snow fell on game day, but it did not stop either high-powered offense. Two quick fourth quarter touchdowns gave Western a 27–21 lead with seven minutes remaining, but All-American running back Jamal Branch punched in a 1-yard touchdown run with a little less that two minutes left to give the Red Raiders a 28–27 win. Colgate advanced to the Division 1AA championship game where dreams of an undefeated season were ended by Delaware.

### 10. NEW YORK GIANTS VERSUS SAN DIEGO

In the final game of the 1995 regular season the Giants played host to the Chargers. Snow had fallen earlier in the week, and although the field was clear, the stands, unfortunately, were not. With the Giants finishing off a miserable season and the game out of reach in the fourth quarter, a bunch of miscreants in the crowd began firing snow and ice balls onto the field—at the Chargers, at the officials, at just about anything that moved. Everybody was a target. And it was not isolated to a couple of fans . . . this turned into an all-out barrage from all corners of Giants Stadium. More than 175 people were ejected, and a Chargers employee was knocked unconscious when he was hit in the head with an ice ball while standing on the sideline. A number of people were arrested, and the Giants took season tickets away from many fans believed to have been involved in the disgusting display.

# These numbers Will never Be Worn Again

These are the men who have gained immortality on the gridiron, the men whose numbers will never again be worn by players on the same team.

## 1. PAT TILLMAN

Pat Tillman played both his college and pro ball in Sun Devil Stadium, and both his college (Arizona State, number 42) and pro (Arizona Cardinals, number 40) uniform numbers hang in the stadium. An intense safety who played with an uncommon drive, Tillman, in 2002, turned down multimillion-dollar contract offers from both the Rams and Cardinals to enlist in the armed forces. After a quick rise to become a member of the elite Army Rangers, Tillman lost his life in the mountains of Afghanistan in 2004.

## 2. JIM BROWn

His career lasted only nine years, but Jim Brown's impact will be felt forever. The man who led the league in rushing eight times, and whose 5.2-yard per carry average is still the best all-time, was also named MVP in both his first two years in the league and his final two years in the league. His number 32 is one of five numbers retired by the Cleveland Browns (along with Otto Graham, Ernie Davis, Don Fleming, and Lou "The Toe" Groza).

## 3. JOHNNY UNITAS

All of his accomplishments were achieved in Baltimore's old Memorial Stadium, but Hall of Famer Johnny Unitas's number 19 is raised in the RCA Dome in Indianapolis, where the Colts now play. If ever one man symbolized a football team, it was Unitas with the Colts. In his seventeen-year Colts career (he also spent one season with the Chargers), Unitas guided them to three world championships (in 1958, 1959, and 1970). He is one of seven Colts to have his number retired, and all seven played their careers in Baltimore.

## 4. JOHN ELWAY

Speaking of players who symbolize a franchise, it's interesting to consider that John Elway nearly didn't become a Denver Bronco. Drafted number 1 overall by the Colts in the 1983 draft, Elway refused to report and forced a trade. He wound up in Denver, and the rest is history. He took the Broncos to five Super Bowls, winning two, and leading countless late-game winning drives. His number 7 joins Floyd Little's 44 and Frank Tripucka's 18 as the only retired numbers in Broncos history.

## 5. DAN FOUTS

Dan Fouts was the perfect quarterback for Don Coryell's pass-oriented offense with the Chargers. With weapons like Kellen Winslow, John Jefferson, Charlie Joyner, and Chuck Muncie, Fouts guided San Diego to the playoffs four times and became the third player in history to pass for more than 40,000 yards. In 1982 he was named the NFL's Most Valuable Player, and his number 14 is the only jersey retired in Chargers history.

## 6. JIM TAYLOR

Hall of Famer Jim Taylor has his jersey number 31 retired, but not by the Green Bay Packers, where he spent his first nine seasons. Taylor won four championships with the Packers, won the MVP in 1962, and had five straight 1,000-yard seasons, but his one season with the expansion New Orleans Saints earned him a retired jersey. Taylor rushed for only 390 yards with the Saints, but he was their marquee player, the one who helped bring some respectability to Tulane Stadium. In the forty-year history of the Saints, only Taylor and Doug Atkins have had their jersey numbers retired.

## 7. STEVE LARGENT

He was small (5 ft. 11 in., 187 pounds) and not exceptionally fast, but Steve Largent had an uncanny ability to find openings in secondaries, and he beat some of the speediest defensive backs down the field. He became the greatest Seattle Seahawk, but only after the Houston Oilers, who drafted him in the fourth round of the 1976 draft gave up on him in the preseason. The Seahawks used an eighth-round pick to trade for one of the ten best wide receivers in history. A three-time All-Pro, number 80 had a streak of 177 straight games with a reception, a record broken by Art Monk and later by Jerry Rice. In 2004 Rice and Largent crossed paths once again, when Rice forced a trade from the Raiders and wound up in Seattle. Rice, who always wore number 80, put Largent in an unenviable position by asking if it would be all right if he wore 80 with the Seahawks. It was not a classy thing to do, but what was Largent supposed to do—say no? Largent's 80 is one of two retired numbers in Seattle, along with number 12. But 12 is not a person; it's for the fans, the team's "twelfth man."

## 8. **THE CHICAGO BEARS**

The Bears have been around since 1920, and no team has honored more players by retiring their numbers. So many greats have manned the gridiron for the home team at both Wrigley Field and Soldier Field that the Bears have immortalized thirteen men with retired jerseys. A member of the Bears will never again wear the following numbers: 3 (Bronko Nagurski), 5 (George McAfee), 7 (George Halas), 28 (Willie Galimore), 34 (Walter Payton), 40 (Gale Sayers), 41 (Brian Piccolo), 42 (Sid Luckman), 51 (Dick Butkus), 56 (Bill Hewitt), 61 (Bill George), 66 (Bulldog Turner), and 77 (Red Grange).

## 9. **DETROIT LIONS NUMBER 20**

During their Thanksgiving 2004 contest versus the Indianapolis Colts, the Lions retired legendary defensive back Lem Barney's number 20. Or was it running back Billy Sims's 20? Or how about Hall of Famer Barry Sanders's 20? Actually, the Lions honored all three. What is surprising is that the Lions recycled the number so often. Barney retired in 1977, and three seasons later Sims made his Lions debut. Sims's career was cut short in 1984 because of a devastating knee injury, and by 1989, Sanders was wearing number 20. Six other Lions have had their numbers retired, but none of them had to share.

## 10. **SAMMY BAUGH**

It's interesting to compare the Washington Redskins to the Chicago Bears. As we noted above, the Bears have retired thirteen jersey numbers in their history, but the Redskins, over more than seventy years, have retired just one: the legendary Sammy Baugh's 33.

# The Grand Gridirons

What's your favorite place to watch a football game? Some stadiums hold such history that it makes a great game an even more memorable one. Here are ten of the best venues in which to watch a football game.

## 1. THE ROSE BOWL

Nestled within the trees of Pasadena, California, sits probably the most famous football stadium in the country. The Rose Bowl opened in 1922 as host of the annual New Year's Day Tournament of Roses game, and has been one of the premier athletic sites for more than eight decades. In addition to hosting more than eighty Rose Bowl battles, it was the site of the 2002 BCS Championship Game, where Miami pummeled Nebraska, and it is also the home facility for the UCLA Bruins. It has played host to five Super Bowls: XI, XIV, XVII, XXI, XXVII. Interestingly, the Rose Bowl was the NFL's first choice to play Super Bowl I, but the Tournament of Roses committee passed on the opportunity.

## 2. THE ORANGE BOWL

A municipal stadium built by the city of Miami in 1937 and almost always glowing in sunshine, the Orange Bowl has been the site of some of the best moments in football history. The venue of the annual Orange Bowl classic until 1996, the facility is still the home of the University of Miami Hurricanes, and from 1966 through 1986 it was the home of the Miami Dolphins. Consider some of the great moments seen in the Orange Bowl: The 1984 Orange Bowl between Nebraska and Miami is recognized as one of the best college football games ever played. A 31–30 Hurricanes win was not decided until the Cornhuskers missed a 2-point conversion opportunity in the closing seconds. Eleven months later, Doug Flutie launched a Hail Mary pass into the Orange Bowl sky and into the history books. Pro football saw Joe Namath's guarantee for the New York Jets in Super Bowl III, the Dolphins perfect season in 1972, two classic Super Bowls between the Steelers and Cowboys, and one of the greatest NFL games ever: the 1981 playoff game where the Chargers beat the Dolphins in overtime.

### 3. NOTRE DAME STADIUM

The most recognizable college football program has one of the most recognizable facilities. Recently expanded to a capacity of more than eighty thousand, Notre Dame Stadium has been the host of Fighting Irish football since 1930, but the most unique feature to a game in South Bend did not appear until 1964. That's when the mural of "Touchdown Jesus" appeared on the Hesburgh Library within walking distance of the stadium, and the mystique of Notre Dame football really took off. Memorable games at Notre Dame Stadium include the 1988 game versus Miami (a 31–30 Notre Dame win) and the back-to-back 1993 games against number one Florida State (a 31–24 Irish win) and Boston College (a 41–38 win for the Eagles).

BOSTON COLLEGE MEDIA RELATIONS DEPARTMENT

Doug Flutie's Hail Mary pass to beat Miami remains one of the
top moments in Orange Bowl stadium history.

## 4. MICHIGAN STADIUM

Seating for 107,501 and nary a ticket to be found. That's the story of the Big House in Ann Arbor, the home of Michigan Wolverine football since 1927. The single-level stadium, modeled after the Yale Bowl, has hosted countless Big Ten battles and was dedicated with a 1927 win over—appropriately—Ohio State, the Wolverines' biggest rival. Since the expansion to its current capacity, Michigan Stadium has seen more than 170 crowds in excess of 100,000.

## 5. MICHIE STADIUM

Nestled within trees high above the banks of the Hudson River sits one of the most breathtaking spots to watch a football game: Michie Stadium on the campus of West Point. Intimate crowds of forty-thousand have gathered for eighty years to watch not only the Black Knights, but also to see the pre-game parade of Cadets, the paratrooper entrance with the game ball, and to hear the cannon blasts following every Army score. Despite recent on-field troubles, the Black Knights still boast an overall winning percentage of more than .700 at Michie.

## 6. LOS ANGELES COLISEUM

Only four stadiums have hosted both the Super Bowl and the World Series: the Metrodome, Joe Robbie Stadium, San Diego (Qualcomm) Stadium, and the Los Angeles Coliseum. Many teams have called the Coliseum home since it opened in 1923: USC has played its home games there from day one; UCLA played in the Coliseum from 1933 through 1981; the Los Angeles Rams called it home from 1946 to 1979; and the Raiders played there from 1982 through 1994. Even the expansion Chargers played there in 1960. The Coliseum was also the site of Super Bowls I and VII, when the Dolphins capped off their magical unbeaten season, and it is the only stadium to have hosted a Super Bowl, an NFC Championship Game, and an AFC Championship Game.

### 7. LAMBEAU FIELD
Home of the Green Bay Packers for forty years, Lambeau Field is one of the most historic stadiums in the NFL. Originally named City Stadium, it was renamed in 1965 after E. L. Lambeau, the Packers founder. Games played there have included many historical moments such as the "Ice Bowl" NFL Championship Game of 1967. Starting with a capacity of 32,000, many renovations later, it now holds more than 60,000.

### 8. ARROWHEAD STADIUM
The Chiefs went from one of the worst stadiums in the NFL to one of the best when they moved out of Municipal Stadium and into Arrowhead, a beautiful three-tiered structure that opened in 1972. It was opened as part of the Truman Athletic Complex and sits alongside Kauffman Stadium, the home of baseball's Royals. Thirty-three years later, Arrowhead is still considered one of the league's top facilities. However, success has eluded the Chiefs since they moved in. They didn't play their first home playoff game at Arrowhead until 1991, and they're still searching for their first Super Bowl championship since 1969.

### 9. LOUISIANA SUPERDOME
Super Bowl IX was held in New Orleans' Tulane Stadium. Where was it supposed to be played? Yes, the Superdome, but construction delays prevented that. The massive dome, with fantastic sight lines, was completed by the next fall, and

it has been the host of six Super Bowls since then, more than any other venue. It was in New Orleans that the Patriots knocked off the Rams in Super Bowl XXXVI on Adam Vinatieri's game-winning field goal.

## 10. **SOLDIER FIELD**

Located near the Field Museum on Chicago's Lake Shore Drive, Soldier Field, with its signature columns, is one of Chicago's architectural landmarks. Originally built in 1925 to hold more than 100,000 spectators, it was best known for years as the site of the College All Star Game, which pitted a team of college all stars against the defending NFL champions. The Bears moved in from Wrigley Field in 1971, when renovations brought capacity down to less than seventy thousand. In 2002, a completely rebuilt and modern Soldier Field opened on the same site. The columns are still there, but now the stands tower over them.

# Small School, Big Career

Every Saturday in the fall, television lineups are full of college football matchups: Miami versus Florida State, Tennessee versus Florida, Michigan versus Iowa—the list goes on and on. Fans become familiar with the bigger schools, so it's no wonder that when the NFL draft rolls around, they let out a little "who?" when a player from a smaller school is taken. But just because a player comes out of a lesser conference does not mean that his worth should be discounted, as the following "small school" players can attest.

### 1. JERRY RICE

In forty-two collegiate games at Mississippi Valley State, Jerry Rice had 310 catches, scoring touchdowns on fifty-one of them. In the 1985 draft Rice was taken by the 49ers with the sixteenth selection, a lofty spot for a player from a small school. But Rice certainly would have gotten higher consideration had he played for, say, Mississippi State instead. In fact, Rice was the third receiver drafted that year, behind Al Toon of Wisconsin and Eddie Brown of the Miami Hurricanes. The personnel men who passed on Rice sure must have had second thoughts now that he's broken just about every receiving record in NFL history.

## 2. WALTER PAYTON

"Sweetness" was Mr. Everything in his college career at Jackson State. In addition to scoring sixty-six touchdowns, Payton handled kicking duties at times, drilling five field goals and fifty-three PATs. In 1975 the Bears made him the fourth overall pick in the draft, and boy was that ever a great pick. Payton finished off a thirteen-year career in 1987 not only as the NFL's all-time leading rusher—with more than 16,000 yards, but also as the Bears all-time leading receiver.

## 3. MEAN JOE GREENE

Joe Greene was a consensus All-American in 1968 despite playing his college ball at North Texas State (not exactly an NFL breeding ground). The Steelers made him their number 1 draft pick in 1969, and he became the anchor of the Steel Curtain. On the way to the Pro Football Hall of Fame, Greene was named NFL Defensive Player of the Year twice, played in ten Pro Bowls, and helped Pittsburgh win four Super Bowls. He had a monster game against Fran Tarkenton and the Vikings in Super Bowl IX, with an interception and a fumble recovery.

## 4. DEACON JONES

Hall of Famer Deacon Jones was the fourteenth round (fourteenth!) selection of the Los Angeles Rams in 1961, and that became one of the best all-time low-round picks. Jones had only played two seasons of college ball, one at South Carolina State and the other at Mississippi Vocational, where the Rams discovered him. He became a master of the sack, a term that he helped coin, as he terrorized quarterbacks over a fourteen-year career. Jones was NFL Defensive Player of the Year twice, All-Pro for six consecutive seasons, played in eight Pro Bowls, *and* he guest starred on *The Brady Bunch, The Odd Couple*, and *Wonder Woman*!

## 5. GENE UPSHAW

Gene Upshaw was the first pick of the Oakland Raiders in the 1967 draft out of Texas A&I—not Texas A&M, but A&I. Upshaw was an NAIA All-American as a senior, and the Raiders liked his potential at the offensive guard spot. Upshaw went on to lead the Raiders to three Super Bowls (in three different decades), winning two of them. Along the way to Canton as the first true guard enshrined in the Hall of Fame, he played in seven Pro Bowls. Today, Upshaw is the head of the NFL Players Association.

## 6. ART SHELL

Gene Upshaw and Art Shell are almost always mentioned in tandem, so why not on this list as well? Shell came to the Raiders one year after Upshaw, a third-round pick out of Maryland Eastern Shore, where he was a 1967 little college All-American. He was a true throwback, playing both ways. An offensive tackle with the Raiders, Shell became a four-time All-Pro who played in eight Pro Bowls and won two Super Bowl rings. In 1989 Shell made history as the NFL's first African-American head coach when he took over the reigns of the Raiders.

## 7. MEL BLOUNT

The second member of the Steelers's dynasty of the 1970s to make this list is defensive back Mel Blount. Taken in the third round of the 1970 draft out of Southern University in Louisiana, Blount became one of the most feared defensive backs of the era: he could cover, he could hit, and he had a knack for finding the ball. During his career, which included five Pro Bowls, Blount accounted for seventy takeaways: fifty-seven interceptions (tied for tenth all time) and thirteen fumble recoveries.

## 8. JOHN STALLWORTH

You get the idea that the Steelers knew what they were doing scouting small-school players. They used their fourth round pick in a historic 1974 draft on John Stallworth, a wide receiver out of Alabama A&M. Why was the draft historic? In the first five rounds, the Steelers drafted four future Hall of Famers: Lynn Swann, Jack Lambert, Stallworth, and Mike Webster. Stallworth was a two-time All-SIAC player who had forty-eight catches and seven touchdowns as a senior. In addition to his four Super Bowl rings, Stallworth made four trips to the Pro Bowl while with the Steelers.

## 9. BULLDOG TURNER

In 1940 players just weren't drafted from schools like Hardin Simmons. The NFL was still fairly young, and most players were taken from big schools. But the Bears found out about Bulldog Turner and made him the first overall pick in the draft, and they would not be disappointed. A fierce competitor who played both center and linebacker, Turner also subbed as a running back later in his career. Bulldog Turner's Hall of Fame career included being named All-NFL for seven seasons.

## 10. JACKIE SMITH

Unfortunately remembered more for a dropped pass for Dallas in Super Bowl XIII than his storied career with the Cardinals, Smith starred in both football and track at NW Louisiana and was taken in the tenth round in 1963 by St. Louis. Following his sixteen-year career, he was the all-time receptions leader among tight ends with 480. Smith played in five Pro Bowls and was twice an All-Pro selection. He was inducted into the Pro Football Hall of Fame in 1994.

# Let's Dance, Baby!

In the three and a half decades since the New York Giants' Homer Jones is believed to be the first player to spike the ball after scoring a touchdown, players have been refining celebrations to a science. Here are some memorable after-touchdown performances.

### 1. THE LAMBEAU LEAP
It only seems that Green Bay Packers have been launching themselves into the stands at Lambeau Field after touchdowns forever. Actually, the tradition began fairly recently. The first to do it was safety Leroy Butler, who jumped into the crowd in 1993 following an interception return. Wide receiver Robert Brooks took note of the reaction of the crowd and began making it a tradition in 1994. Now it's rare to see a Packer score and not take a "leap" into the crowd.

### 2. THE FUNKY CHICKEN: WHITE SHOES JOHNSON
Billy "White Shoes" Johnson, a wide receiver and kick returner for the Oilers and Falcons, had probably the most memorable individual touchdown celebration, which came to be known as the Funky Chicken. Holding his arms up in the air, Johnson would scissor-kick both legs, then roll the

ball down his arm and behind his neck. This is the dance against which all others should be measured.

### 3. THE FUN BUNCH

The high-powered Redskins' offense of the early 1980s had a lot to celebrate, and one of the ways they did it was with a group high-five. After most Washington touchdown receptions, the receivers (a.k.a. The Fun Bunch) would gather in the back of the end zone in a circle, jump, and high-five. The league banished the move in 1984, after scuffles broke out when opposing players tried to intervene.

### 4. THE ICKEY SHUFFLE

How does one begin to describe The Ickey Shuffle? Three steps left, three steps right, bounce back three steps on one foot, and spike? A verbal description doesn't do it justice. Ickey Woods burst on the scene in 1988 as a star rookie back with the Cincinnati Bengals, and after every score he would do his shuffle. Woods definitely got an "A" for originality, as this was almost impossible to duplicate.

### 5. TERRELL OWENS

Terrell goes into the touchdown celebration hall of fame for his ability to be original, spontaneous, and infuriating. First, there was the game in Dallas, where he scored twice, and each time he tried to spike the ball on the star at midfield. His final attempt was interrupted by a tackle from Cowboys' safety George Teague. Then, of course, there was the touchdown at Candlestick Park, after which he borrowed pom poms from a cheerleader and did a little dance. But no Terrell moment tops the Sharpie. After a touchdown catch in Seattle against the Seahawks, Owens stooped down and pulled out a pen from his sock, then signed the ball and handed it to one of his representatives in a box behind the end zone.

## 6. BUTCH JOHNSON

The Cowboys' receiver called his celebration The California Quake, though it's not altogether clear where that name came from. After every touchdown, Johnson would get into an exaggerated squat, point both hands like they were pistols, blast away, then put his "guns" back into his "holster."

## 7. JOE HORN

Just a few weeks after Terrell Owens celebrated with a Sharpie, Saints receiver Joe Horn did him one better. After scoring a touchdown during a game at the Superdome, Horn raced to the goalpost. He then lifted the foam padding to remove an object underneath, which turned out to be a cell phone. He punched in numbers and pretended to have a conversation. Clever, yes. But he loses points for his lack of spontaneity, since the stunt was so obviously premeditated.

## 8. RANDY MOSS

During a playoff game at Lambeau Field following the 2004 season, the Vikings' Moss caught a touchdown pass from Daunte Culpepper. Eschewing simply spiking the ball, Moss rubbed it in to the Packer faithful by rushing to the goal post, mock-dropping his pants, and rubbing his rear end against the padding. This one definitely added insult to injury to Green Bay fans, who had to watch this and then watch their team get beaten.

## 9. ALFRED PUPUNU

The tight end for the Chargers, originally from Samoa, had a unique way to celebrate his scores. Pupunu would pretend to cut open the top of the ball and drink the contents, like it was a coconut. Pupunu's biggest touchdown was probably a score in the 1994 AFC Championship Game against Pittsburgh, a win that propelled the Chargers to their only Super Bowl.

## 10. ELMO WRIGHT

The former University of Houston wide receiver was a visionary of sorts. In 1973, while playing for the Chiefs, he caught a touchdown pass from Len Dawson and did a little dance in the end zone before spiking the ball. This is widely recognized as the first end zone dance . . . but it clearly was not the last.

# Draft Flops

One of the few consolations for fans of bad pro teams is the opportunity for a high selection in the NFL draft. Many times, teams get players who become foundations to the franchise. Take the 1965 Bears, for example. They had two first-round draft picks, a couple of fellas you may have heard of: Dick Butkus and Gale Sayers. Or, more recently, there were the Baltimore Ravens of 1996. They had two first-round picks and took quite possibly two future Hall of Famers: Jonathan Ogden and Ray Lewis. But being a first-round pick in the draft does not ensure NFL success, as these ten players can attest.

### 1. TOM COUSINEAU

With the first overall pick in the 1979 draft, the Buffalo Bills chose Tom Cousineau, a two-time All-American linebacker from Ohio State. Cousineau set a Buckeyes single season record for tackles, and the Bills thought they had someone to stabilize their defense for years to come. However, Cousineau signed with the CFL and never played a down in Buffalo. In 1982 he signed with the Browns, where he played four undistinguished years, before he finished out his career with the 49ers for two seasons. For his six-year career,

Cousineau recorded ten interceptions and just 6.5 sacks. Some of the notables taken in the top fifteen after Cousineau that year: Dan Hampton, Phil Simms, O. J. Anderson, Kellen Winslow, and Marty Lyons.

## 2. TONY MANDARICH

As an offensive tackle at Michigan State, Tony Mandarich dominated opposing defensive lines. Some said he could become the best tackle that ever played the game. He was blessed with size and speed, made the cover of *Sports Illustrated* (that should have been an omen), and became the second overall pick in the 1989 draft by the Green Bay Packers. But Mandarich, hampered by poor play, alleged attitude problems, and (loud) whispers about possible steroid use, played just three years in Green Bay before being cut. Mandarich resurfaced with the Indianapolis Colts, with whom he started for a few years. Mandarich was a colossal bust not just because of how bad he turned out to be, but because of who was picked around him. Here's how the top five of that draft looked: Troy Aikman, Mandarich, Barry Sanders, Derrick Thomas, Deion Sanders.

## 3. BLAIR THOMAS

For the Jets, the second pick in the 1990 draft was a slam dunk: veteran running back Freeman McNeil could no longer handle a role as the every down back, and waiting in their draft slot was the consensus among NFL staff as the best running back. New coach Bruce Coslet would be blessed with a franchise back to build the team around. The only problem was that Blair Thomas never did much. He couldn't hit the holes, and he became a bust. In his second year he rushed for 728 yards, which isn't terrible, but it is about half of what you would expect a high pick to average each year. Oh, and another thing that bothers Jets fans to this day about the pick: The next running back selected went off the board at number 17 to the Dallas Cowboys—Emmitt Smith.

### 4. AUNDRAY BRUCE

The Atlanta Falcons took Aundray Bruce, a linebacker out of Auburn, with the number 1 pick of the 1988 draft, but Bruce never played like the second coming of Lawrence Taylor. Yes, he did have a pretty long career with the Falcons (four seasons) and Raiders (seven years), but he was never a dominant force. The best players selected in the first round in 1988 turned out to be wide receivers Tim Brown, Sterling Sharpe, and Michael Irvin.

### 5. TODD MARINOVICH

He was not a high first-round pick, but any time a quarterback goes anywhere in the first round and doesn't succeed, he's a flop. The media touted him as "Robo-QB" through his recruitment to Southern California. Marinovich's father, Marv, had been working with Todd since he was a boy, controlling his environment. Marv's influence was so great that it was said Todd had never even had a cheeseburger. Todd played two years at USC and that was enough for Al Davis, who drafted him to play pro ball in the same stadium as his college home. Marinovich, free of his father's control, became somewhat of a free spirit—and he also became fond of marijuana. Marinovich played just eight regular season games over two years with the Raiders, plus a dreadful playoff loss to the Chiefs in 1991, where he threw four interceptions.

### 6. AKILI SMITH

Many have called Tim Couch, the number one overall pick in 1999 by the Browns, a bust for his largely forgettable career in Cleveland, but the guy picked two spots behind Couch turned out to be an even bigger flop. Akili Smith came out of Oregon as a strong-armed gunslinger, and the Cincinnati Bengals hoped Smith was the guy to bring them back to the postseason for the first time since Boomer Esiason was their quarterback. Smith played in just twenty-one games for the Bengals over four seasons. Remarkably, or unbelievably, he threw just five touchdown passes in his career. Five touchdown passes made for a good *game* for Esiason. So who did the Bengals leave on the draft board? Edgerrin James, Ricky Williams, Daunte Culpepper, Torry Holt, and Jevon Kearse, just to name a few.

## 7. RYAN LEAF

We were bound to get around to Ryan Leaf, no? When the 1998 draft came around, the big question for the Indianapolis Colts was Ryan Leaf or Peyton Manning? They went with Manning, and let's just say that was a good pick. The Chargers were not so lucky selecting second. Everyone thought Leaf had a good arm, but they had some concerns about his maturity. Those concerns certainly manifested themselves during a career of terrible play, temper tantrums, and suspensions. In Leaf's rookie year, he totaled an incomprehensible two touchdowns and fifteen interceptions.

## 8. ART SCHLICHTER

After a dreadful 1981 season, the Baltimore Colts looked for a quarterback in the draft to replace incumbent veteran Bert Jones, and with the fourth selection they thought they had their guy: Ohio State's Art Schlichter. The Bears, picking fifth, also took a quarterback: BYU's Jim McMahon. Well, we all know who got the better of those picks. Schlichter played in just thirteen games over three seasons, thanks to gambling trouble. The Colts had to go back to the drawing board one year later when they took another quarterback, John Elway with the first overall pick. Elway refused to sign with the team. Incidentally, the Colts leading rusher in 1982 was a guy named Randy McMillan. I only mention this because a pretty good back was on the board when the Colts selected him: Marcus Allen, who went eleventh to the Raiders.

### 9. TODD BLACKLEDGE

It was known as the great quarterback class of 1983—six signal callers were taken in the first round. Now that we can look back at each of the six's respective careers, let's not call it a great class. Let's say three were great (John Elway, Dan Marino, Jim Kelly), two were middling (Ken O'Brien, Tony Eason), and one didn't work out at all: Todd Blackledge, who was taken seventh overall by the Kansas City Chiefs. Blackledge was just a part-time starter throughout his seven-year career, spending many of his Kansas City years backing up the immortal Bill Kenney. In addition to passing on Marino, Kelly, Eason, and O'Brien, the Chiefs also could have had Bruce Matthews or Darrell Green.

### 10. KELLY STOUFFER

The Seattle Seahawks had a good run of quarterbacking early in their history, with Jim Zorn and Dave Kreig ably running the team. In 1987 the Seahawks looked for Kreig's successor in the draft. Instead, with the number 7 pick, they got Kelly Stouffer. Stouffer played just parts of four seasons with Seattle. Looking past the fact that they overlooked future Hall of Famer Rod Woodson and stud defensive tackle Jerome Brown, they could have had either of two other first-round quarterbacks who had serviceable NFL careers: Chris Miller and Jim Harbaugh.

# Heisman Flops

Every year, the Downtown Athletic Club awards the Heisman Trophy to the nation's best college football player. That moment should be the launching point to a fine professional career, right? Well, not necessarily, as the following winners and candidates demonstrate.

## 1. ERIC CROUCH

A true option quarterback, the dynamic Crouch led the Nebraska Cornhuskers to the 2001 BCS Championship Game, where they were soundly defeated by the Miami Hurricanes. Along the way, Crouch ran for more than 1,100 yards and eighteen touchdowns and threw for more than 1,500 yards and seven touchdowns. He even scored on a dramatic 63-yard touchdown reception against arch-rival Oklahoma. NFL scouts never saw Crouch as a quarterback at the pro level, but he was drafted by the St. Louis Rams, who hoped Crouch could use his speed to convert to wide receiver. But that never happened, as Crouch retired during his inaugural training camp. He later hooked up with Green Bay and Kansas City, but he never got his pro career off the ground.

## 2. CHRIS WEINKE

Chris Weinke won the 2000 Heisman Trophy at Florida State as a 28-year-old senior (he had played minor league baseball before enrolling in college) who took the Seminoles to their second consecutive BCS Championship Game, where they were thumped by Oklahoma 13–2 (after winning the national championship the previous year with a Sugar Bowl win over Virginia Tech). Weinke was drafted by the Carolina Panthers in the fourth round of the 2001 draft and was installed immediately as the starter. He threw for only 11 touchdowns with nineteen interceptions, as the Panthers went 1–15. He lost his job the following season to Rodney Peete, and he continued as a backup for four seasons behind Peete and, later, Jake Delhomme.

## 3. RON DAYNE

Dayne won the 1999 Heisman Trophy for the Wisconsin Badgers, and the New York Giants felt the bruising back could become a dominant NFL player and took him in the first round. Dayne was serviceable, but by no means was he dominant in his first two years as a pro, rushing for 770 yards as a rookie and 690 yards in his second year. He often found himself in head coach Jim Fassel's doghouse and saw his playing time diminish as Tiki Barber established himself as the number one back. Dayne fell so low that he was inactive for the entire 2003 season. Following the 2004 season, he was picked up by the Broncos in an attempt to resurrect his career.

## 4. DANNY WUERFFEL

Wuerffel had one of the great careers in NCAA history, as his Florida teams had a 46–6–1 record in his four years, and he threw for more than ten thousand yards. Wuerffel and his rocket arm led the Gators to the national championship game twice, winning one. He won the Heisman in 1996 and was drafted by the New Orleans Saints, but he lasted only four years in the NFL, throwing for just 2,123 yards, twelve touchdowns, and twenty-two picks. The best NFL player among the Heisman finalists in 1996? Offensive tackle Orlando Pace of Ohio State, who quickly established himself as one of the best linemen in the league.

## 5. RASHAAN SALAAM

In 1994 Salaam became just the fourth collegiate back to rush for 2,000 yards in a season for the Colorado Buffaloes, including 312 in one game versus Texas. This made him an easy selection for the Heisman Trophy over Penn State's Ki-Jana Carter. Salaam became the first-round selection of the Chicago Bears, and after a holdout, he had five 100-yard rushing games on his way to a 1,074-yard season. Injuries marred his career from that point forward, as he played in parts of just two more seasons with the Bears.

## 6. CHARLIE WARD

Okay, it's hard to call Charlie Ward a bust. In addition to playing quarterback at Florida State, Ward started in a backcourt with Sam Cassell for the basketball team, and he was a pro prospect in both sports. But when you win a Heisman Trophy and never even take a crack at playing in the NFL, what label do you get? Ward never played in the NFL, but he was drafted and contributed to some fine New York Knicks teams in the NBA. In fact, early in his New York career, as the Jets struggled with Boomer Esiason and the Giants were led by Dave Brown, the running joke in the city was that the best quarterback in town played for the Knicks.

## 7. **PAT SULLIVAN**

Sullivan, a quarterback for Auburn, won a close Heisman race with Cornell running back Ed Marinaro (best remembered today as Joe Coffey on *Hill Street Blues*), taking the trophy by just 142 points. Marinaro actually won the voting in three of the five regions, but Sullivan had a big edge in the South. Sullivan's pro career lasted just four seasons with the Atlanta Falcons, where he served as a backup to such stars as Bob Berry and Bob Lee.

## 8. **RYAN LEAF**

The 1997 Heisman race was considered one of the best ever. Of the top five vote-getters, two are NFL all-time greats (Peyton Manning, who finished second, and Randy Moss, who was fourth in the voting), two became very gifted NFL players (winner Charles Woodson, and fifth-place finisher Ricky Williams), and one was a bust of enormous proportions. Washington State's Ryan Leaf, who many looked at as a fiery, strong-armed leader, instead was an immature, unsteady-in-the-pocket flop, who was out of the NFL after just a few seasons.

## 9. **HEATH SHULER**

We've already discussed Charlie Ward, the winner of the 1993 trophy, but what about the second-place finisher, Heath Shuler? Drafted in the first round out of the University of Tennessee by the Redskins, he never lived up to his potential, losing his job at one point to fellow rookie Gus Frerotte. But look at the rest of the Heisman finalists that year, and you'll find a collection of NFL stiffs. Of the ten finalists, nine never amounted to much as a pro. The tenth is a surefire Hall of Famer, fourth-place finisher Marshall Faulk of San Diego State. Here is how the rest of the top ten shook out: David Palmer of

Alabama was third, Glenn Foley of Boston College was fifth, LeShon Johnson of Northern Illinois was sixth, J.J. Stokes of UCLA was seventh, Michigan's Tyrone Wheatley was eighth, Trent Dilfer of Fresno State was ninth, and Georgia's Eric Zeier was tenth.

## 10. PAUL PALMER

Running back Paul Palmer of Temple finished second to Vinny Testaverde of Miami in the 1986 Heisman balloting, but he did very little when he moved on to the NFL. Palmer played only three years, rushing for just 1,053 yards in two seasons with the Chiefs and one with the Cowboys.

# Diamonds In The Draft Rough

Usually when a team targets a player in the first or second round of the NFL draft, they expect him to be a contributor. As you get into the later rounds, the picks become more of a crapshoot, but that doesn't mean teams don't find great players in the latter stages of the draft. Here are ten players from this generation who were overlooked early but turned into outstanding NFL players.

### 1. TOM BRADY
Quarterback Tom Brady out of the University of Michigan was New England's sixth-round pick in the 2000 draft. You wonder how much the Patriots' braintrust thought of him at first, because, for a time as a rookie, he was fourth on the depth chart. By the time 2001 rolled around, Brady was the backup to Drew Bledsoe, and when Bledsoe went down to injury in week two, Brady became the starter. The rest is history: three Super Bowl championships in four years, a feat matched only by Troy Aikman.

### 2. TERRELL DAVIS
The Denver Broncos chose running back Terrell Davis from

UNIVERSITY OF GEORGIA ATHLETIC ASSOCIATION

Georgia running back Terrell Davis went undrafted until the sixth
round being picked by the Broncos.

Georgia as their sixth-round selection in 1995, and Davis became an immediate star. Before injuries derailed his career, Davis had four straight 1,000-yard seasons, including a 2,008-yard, twenty-one-touchdown campaign in 1998. It's no coincidence that the Broncos had one of the great three-season stretches during Davis's peak years: From 1996 through 1998, the Broncos went 46–10 (including postseason) and won two Super Bowls.

### 3. SHANNON SHARPE
Here is another late-round selection that helped the Broncos win back-to-back Super Bowls in 1997 and 1998. Tight end Shannon Sharpe was picked in the seventh round out of Savannah State. All Sharpe did in a fourteen-year career was become one of the elite pass-catching tight ends in the game, go to eight Pro Bowls, and win three Super Bowls.

### 4. RICHARD DENT
Richard Dent, one of the premier pass-rushing defensive ends of all time, slipped all the way to the eighth round of the 1983 draft where he was picked by the Chicago Bears. He became a vital member of Buddy Ryan's great Bear defenses of the 1980s, and he terrorized the Patriots offense on his way to earning MVP honors in Super Bowl XX. Dent played fifteen years in the NFL and went to four Pro Bowls. He recorded 141 career sacks, an average of more than nine per season.

### 5. JAMAL ANDERSON
The Atlanta Falcons probably didn't realize that their seventh-round pick in 1994 would play such a vital role in their improbable march to the Super Bowl four years later, but that's just what Jamal Anderson did. In the Falcons' 14–2 season in

1998 Anderson led the NFL in rushing with 1,846 yards. Injuries curtailed his career soon thereafter, but there's no questioning his importance to a great Falcons team.

### 6. ZACH THOMAS

At Texas Tech Zach Thomas got a reputation as a guy who could make plays from the middle linebacker spot. But he was only 5 ft. 11 in. and 230 pounds, which probably scared away some NFL scouts. That's why he lasted to the fifth round of the 1996 draft, where he was selected by Jimmy Johnson and the Miami Dolphins. Boy, did Thomas prove the "experts" wrong about his size. He became an instant starter as a rookie and has started for ten years. For his career, Thomas has averaged 9.5 tackles per game.

### 7. LEON LETT

Thanks to the Herschel Walker trade in 1989, the Cowboys were able to stockpile draft picks in the early 1990s, which enabled them to take a few more chances than other teams. And that's just what they did in the seventh round in 1991, taking little-known defensive tackle Leon Lett. Lett became one of the standouts of the Cowboys' dynasty, making two Pro Bowls in his eleven-year career. But he's best known for two bonehead plays: getting stripped by the Bills' Don Beebe in Super Bowl XXVII; and trying to jump on a blocked field goal attempt by the Dolphins' Pete Stoyanovich on Thanksgiving Day 1993, which ultimately led to a last-second Dolphins win.

### 8. KEVIN GREENE

The Los Angeles Rams made Greene their eighth-round pick in 1985, and he quickly paid dividends, helping the team to the NFC championship game as a rookie. Greene would go on to a fifteen-year career for four teams, in which he'd appear in five Pro Bowls.

### 9. JESSIE ARMSTEAD

Despite a great college career at one of the premier programs (Miami), Jessie Armstead fell to the eighth round of the 1993 draft. That may have been due to being smaller than the average NFL linebacker, but Armstead became a vital cog in Giants' defenses that helped win NFC East championships in 1997 and 2000. Over a twelve-year career, he played ten with the Giants and another two with the Redskins.

### 10. MARK CLAYTON

The Miami Dolphins struck gold in the 1983 draft when Dan Marino fell to them at the end of the first round. But they also found another gem in the eighth round, wide receiver Mark Clayton, who would become one of Marino's favorite targets. Thanks in large part to his Hall of Fame quarterback, Clayton posted five 1,000-yard receiving seasons, and four years with seventy-plus receptions. In 1984 Clayton led the NFL in touchdown receptions with eighteen. He led the league again in 1988, when he scored fourteen times.

# Super Streaks

There are times when teams and players get on such a roll that it seems they'll never be stopped. Here are nine of the greatest streaks in football history, and one that was not so great.

### 1. OKLAHOMA

In 1953 Oklahoma lost a game to Notre Dame 28–21, then played Pittsburgh for a tie. The following week, Oklahoma topped arch rival Texas 19–14, and a storied winning streak was born. The Sooners did not lose for another four years, as they racked up win after win—forty-seven in total. The most storied winning streak in college football history came to an end in 1957 when Notre Dame—the last team to defeat Oklahoma—upset the Sooners 7–0 in Norman.

### 2. MIAMI DOLPHINS

From the final game of the 1971 season to the second game of the 1973 regular season, the Miami Dolphins did not lose a regular, or postseason game. In all, they won twenty-two straight games, including the perfect 1972 season. Their streak came to an end with a 12–7 loss in Oakland to the Raiders.

### 3. NEW ENGLAND PATRIOTS

In 2003 the Patriots stood at 2–2 after a loss to the Redskins in Washington, but they started winning after that and didn't stop. New England won all twelve remaining regular season games, survived scares from Tennessee in the playoffs and Carolina in the Super Bowl, then won their first six regular season games in 2004. Their win over the Jets in New England gave the Pats twenty-one consecutive wins, but the streak was snapped the following week in Pittsburgh.

### 4. JERRY RICE

Rice holds almost all individual receiving records in NFL history, but through his long career he kept up a remarkable streak: pass receptions in 274 regular season games—the equivalent of a little more than sixteen regular seasons. His streak actually began in his rookie year of 1985 and ended in 2004, when the 42-year-old Rice, playing for the Raiders, did not have a reception in a win over the Bills.

### 5. JIM MARSHALL

He may be remembered as one of the fierce Purple People Eaters of the Minnesota Vikings' defense. He may be remembered as the guy who ran into the wrong end zone with a fumble. But he will also be recalled as one of the NFL's true Iron Men. From his rookie season in Cleveland in 1960 through nineteen seasons in Minnesota, Marshall played in a mind-boggling 282 consecutive games, a feat exceeded only by punter Jeff Feagles, who played in 288 games through the 2005 season.

### 6. JOHNNY UNITAS

What Joe DiMaggio's fifty-six-game hitting streak is to baseball, Johnny Unitas's forty-seven consecutive games with at least one touchdown pass is to the NFL. In the final game of his rookie year (1956), Unitas began the streak. It continued through 1957 (when he was the league's MVP), 1958 and 1959 (back-to-back championship seasons for Baltimore), and extended into 1960, where the streak was stopped by the Los Angeles Rams in the Coliseum. Unitas's record is all the more amazing when you realize that the next closest streak is thirty games by Dan Marino. Third on the list, believe it or not, is Dave Krieg, with twenty-eight.

### 7. LENNY MOORE

The fleet Moore, a teammate of Unitas's with Baltimore, holds the record for consecutive regular season games scoring a touchdown. Moore's streak of eighteen straight games ran from 1963 through 1965, a feat later matched by LaDainian Tomlinson (see below).

### 8. MORTEN ANDERSEN

The ageless Morten Andersen has scored at least one point in every game he's played since the 1983 season. That's 332 consecutive games. To put into perspective how incredible this is, consider that only two other players in history have even *played* more than 332 games (George Blanda and Gary Anderson), and that the next guy on the list is former Bengals kicker Jim Breech, who scored in 186 straight games.

### 9. LaDAINIAN TOMLINSON

Over the course of the 2004 and 2005 NFL seasons, there was no better running back in the NFL than the Chargers' LaDainian Tomlinson. During those seasons, he scored rushing touchdowns in eighteen consecutive games, shattering the old record of 13, held by former Redskins George Rogers and John Riggins.

## 10. TAMPA BAY BUCCANEERS

If Oklahoma, the Dolphins, and the Patriots are the good, then the Tampa Bay Buccaneers of 1976 and 1977 are the bad and ugly, combined. The Buccaneers lost the first twenty-six games of their franchise's existence and were two losses shy of back-to-back winless years. But on the thirteenth week of the 1977 season, something remarkable happened. An inspired Tampa Bay defense recorded touchdowns on three interception returns, and they beat the Saints in the Superdome 33–14. To top it off, they beat St. Louis the next week to finish 2–12, and put the 26-game streak behind them. And put it behind them they did, as they made the NFC Championship Game just two seasons later.

# "They're Not Yelling Boo!"

Boos are raining down from the crowd . . . or are they? When these men took the field, you just never knew.

## 1. MOOSE JOHNSTON

The fullback for Dallas's three championship teams of the 1990s, the Moose was one of the most popular Cowboys to their legion of fans. In fact, whenever he touched the ball during his eleven-year career—at home or on the road—the chants of "Moose" could be deafening.

## 2. ISAAC BRUCE

The chorus of "Bruuuce" has echoed through the Edward Jones Dome in St. Louis since it opened in 1995, whenever wide receiver Isaac Bruce makes a play. Bruce, whose career with the Rams stretches back to when they played in Los Angeles, has played in four Pro Bowls in eleven seasons. He had one of the greatest seasons ever for a receiver when he hauled in 119 passes in 1995, but he is perhaps best remembered for catching the championship-clinching, 73-yard touchdown pass from Kurt Warner in Super Bowl XXXIV.

### 3. JOHN MATUSZAK

The wild man of the Raiders defensive line from 1976 through 1981, the "Tooz" became a huge favorite in Raider Nation. He led the Raiders to two Super Bowl titles, and his popularity was so sky-high that his autobiography, *Cruisin' with the Tooz*, became a national bestseller.

### 4. AL TOON

In 1985 it looked like there were two superstar rookie wide receivers: Jerry Rice of the 49ers and Al Toon of the Jets. In fact, Jets fans had many opportunities to shout "Toooon." He had ninety-three receptions to lead the league in 1988, but Toon was forced to retire after eight seasons due to complications from a series of concussions.

### 5. TONY SIRAGUSA

The mammoth defensive tackle and funnyman was serenaded with "Goose" after a big play. The Goose played twelve NFL seasons with the Colts and Ravens and was a member of the 2000 Super Bowl champion Ravens defense. Following retirement, he dabbled in acting (including a couple of guest appearances on *The Sopranos*), then he joined FOX as an analyst, ironically working on the same broadcast team with another member of this list: Moose Johnston.

### 6. DEUCE McALISTER

Drafted by the Saints in 2001 out of Ole Miss, McAlister had his breakout season the following year, when he rushed for thirteen touchdowns, giving the Superdome crowd plenty of reasons to scream "Deuce." He followed up that season with 1,641 yards on the ground in 2003.

## 7. BOO WILLIAMS

The 2001 draft was a gold mine for Saints fans who like to yell. First McAlister, then Williams. But in this case, the fans really *were* yelling "Boo." Through his first four years with New Orleans, Boo Williams averaged twenty-six receptions per season.

## 8. DUCE STALEY

Philadelphia has some of the loudest fans in the NFL, and they saved some of their most vociferous moments to cheer on "Duuuuce." Through seven seasons with the team, he helped guide the Eagles to three conference championship games. His best season was in 2002 when he rushed for 1,029 yards and had sixty-three receptions. In 2004 he signed with Pittsburgh and had 830 yards on the ground for the 15–1 Steelers.

## 9. DREW BENNETT

The crowd at Adelphia Coliseum in Nashville discovered a new fan favorite in 2004, as wide receiver Drew Bennett had his breakout year. Thanks to eleven touchdown receptions, Titans fans had plenty of reasons to shout "Drew."

## 10. BRUCE SMITH

The number 1 overall pick in 1995, defensive end Bruce Smith introduced Buffalo fans to a new chant: "Bruuuce." Over the course of a sure-to-be-Hall-of-Fame, nineteen-year career (with the Bills and Redskins), Smith set the NFL record for career sacks, finishing with two hundred.

# not You Again

Rivalries make college football exciting, especially late sea-son matchups with championship implications, such as Michigan versus Ohio State and Florida versus Florida State. But it's not just the powerhouse schools that have big rival-ries. These are the ten most-played matchups in college foot-ball.

### 1. LAFAYETTE–LEHIGH
Separated by about fifteen miles in eastern Pennsylvania, Pa-triot League rivals Lafayette and Lehigh have played each other every year since 1884. Through 2005, they'd played 141 times and the Leopards of Lafayette held a 74–62–5 lead over the Mountain Hawks. Lafayette's 2004 victory gave them the Patriot League championship.

### 2. YALE–PRINCETON
Traditional Ivy rivals Yale and Princeton first met on the grid-iron in 1873—to put that in some perspective, football was invented in 1869. So these two have been competing almost since the birth of the game. In 128 matchups, Yale has won seventy times to Princeton's forty-eight, with ten ties.

BRENT HUGO, SPECIALTY PHOTOGRAPHIC, INC.

Lehigh and Lafayette tangle in one of college football's
oldest rivalries.

### 3. **YALE–HARVARD**

It's long been known simply as "The Game." When Yale and Harvard meet on the football field, national championships are not usually on the line, but this game is about more than just bragging rights. Each team would take delight in going 1–10, if they knew the one win would be over their rival. Since 1875, they've played 122 times, with Yale holding a 64–50–8 advantage.

### 4. **MINNESOTA–WISCONSIN**

The winner of the annual Minnesota–Wisconsin football game is awarded Paul Bunyan's Ax, and Wisconsin is the team that has brought it home the most. The Badgers and Golden Gophers have met 115 times since their initial showdown in 1890, and the Badgers have won sixty-one games to the Golden Gophers forty-six, with eight contests ending in ties.

### 5. **RICHMOND–WILLIAM & MARY**

These two Virginia schools have met 115 times, and it's usually the final game of the regular season. Known as the I–64 Bowl since 1984, the Tribe from William and Mary have the upper hand, winning fifty-nine games to the Spiders' fifty-one, with five ties.

### 6. **KANSAS–MISSOURI**

In 114 matchups through the 2005 season, Kansas holds a narrow 53–52–9 edge over Missouri. The Jayhawks and Tigers play for the Indian War Drum. The game had been called The Border War for a number of years, but it was recently changed to The Border Showdown, while real war raged in the Middle East.

## 7. PENN-CORNELL

There's some dispute on the overall record between these two Ivy League institutions. Through 2005, they had played 112 times, and Penn held a commanding 64–42–5 advantage over Cornell. But the Quakers claim that they've won sixty-five and lost only forty-one. Since 1995, the teams have battled over The Trustees Cup.

## 8. TEXAS-TEXAS A&M

Usually played on Thanksgiving weekend, you will seldom experience a more intense rivalry than Texas versus Texas A&M. Through 112 games, the Longhorns have dominated the Aggies in the game that's come to be known as The Lone Star Showdown, winning seventy-three while losing only thirty-four and tying five.

## 9. CINCINNATI-MIAMI (OH)

Of the rivalries on this list, this is the only one in which the two schools are not in the same conference. The Bearcats of the Big East and the Redhawks of the MAC have met 109 times, with The Victory Bell on the line. For the overall series, Miami has the edge, having won fifty-nine, while losing just forty-four and tying seven times.

## 10. NORTH CAROLINA-VIRGINIA

The most-played rivalry in the ACC is somewhat surprisingly not between any of the four schools in North Carolina. Instead, it involves the Tar Heels and the Cavaliers of Virginia. In 110 meetings through 2005, the Heels hold the advantage in the series winning fifty-six times to Virginia's forty-nine, with four games ending in a tie.

# Why Do We Keep Playing These Guys?

Rivalries are a great part of the college football experience. Teams battle it out against one another every season, usually due to conference affiliation, but sometimes not. There are some rivalries in which one team doesn't live up to its end of the bargain and becomes a perennial whipping boy for its opponent. Here are the ten longest losing streaks by one school against another.

## 1. NAVY VERSUS NOTRE DAME
The Midshipmen and the Fighting Irish play each other every season. So how long has it been since Navy beat Notre Dame? Well, Kennedy was in the White House, the Beatles had yet to arrive in the United States, and Roger Staubach was their quarterback. The year was 1963. Since then, the Middies have lost forty-two straight to the Irish, the longest such streak in NCAA history. Navy has played the games close recently, especially in South Bend, losing their last three games in Notre Dame Stadium by just four, four, and three points.

## 2. KANSAS VERSUS NEBRASKA
In 1968 Kansas knocked off Nebraska in Lincoln by a score

of 23–13. Since then, the Jayhawks have been humbled time and again by the Cornhuskers, and the rivalry has featured a number of blowouts for Nebraska, with scores like 70–0, 67–13, 54–2, and 63–10. There have been a few close games, though, like the 1973 contest that ended in a 10–9 Nebraska win, and the 1993 game in Lawrence that the Jayhawks lost just 21–20. But in 2005, the Jayhawks finally broke the streak, toppling the Cornhuskers 40–15 in Lawrence.

### 3. KANSAS STATE VERSUS OKLAHOMA

In 1934 the Wildcats of Kansas State knocked off Oklahoma 8–7, and two years later the two teams played to a 6–6 tie. But starting in 1937, the Sooners would beat K State for thirty-two consecutive seasons. And beat them they did. In one fifteen-year stretch from 1948 through 1962, Oklahoma shut out the Wildcats ten times and outscored them by a combined 584–32! That's an average score of 39–2. Finally, in 1969, Kansas State exacted some revenge, with a 59–21 thumping to end the streak.

### 4. KANSAS STATE VERSUS NEBRASKA

Look, it's the Wildcats again! The same year they ended their futility against Oklahoma, they began a long losing streak against another conference rival, Nebraska. The previous season, K State had knocked off Nebraska in Lincoln by a score of 12–0, and it was not until 1997—a span of twenty-nine games—before they would beat them again. Along the way, Nebraska threw a few of its trademark beatings the Wildcats' way, to the tunes of 59–7, 49–3, and 56–3. By the time 1997 rolled around, Bill Snyder had built the Kansas State program into a national power, and they were ranked number 2 in the country when they beat Nebraska 40–30 in Manhattan before a national television audience.

### 5. VIRGINIA VERSUS CLEMSON

Between 1955 and 1990, Clemson knocked off its ACC rival Virginia twenty-nine consecutive times. Included in that stretch was a 47–0 thumping in 1959. The Cavaliers did not end the streak until 1990, when they were in the midst of a 7–0 start that catapulted them to a number 1 national ranking. Virginia beat the Tigers 20–7 that season.

### 6. RICE VERSUS TEXAS

The former Southwest Conference rivals met every season, and the Longhorns traditionally came out on top. From 1966 through 1994, Texas beat Rice twenty-eight consecutive times. But in 1994, just two seasons before the SWC broke up, the Owls sprung a 19–17 upset on a rainy Sunday night at Rice Stadium in front of a national television audience.

### 7. HOBART VERSUS SYRACUSE

The two upstate New York schools no longer meet on the football field, as Hobart stopped playing major college football years ago, but it's probably just as well. Syracuse held a dominant advantage in the rivalry, winning twenty-six consecutive games between 1906 and 1931.

### 8. OREGON STATE VERSUS USC

In 1967 Oregon State had a pretty special season. Their final record was 7–2–1, which doesn't seem all that great at first glance. However, during that season, they were giant-killers. They beat Purdue when the Boilermakers were ranked number 2 in the country, then they tied UCLA when the Bruins were number 2, then, late in the season, they upset number 1 USC and O.J. Simpson 3–0 in Corvallis. It was enough to earn the Beavers the number 7 ranking in the final polls. But it would be a long time before they celebrated another vicit would be a long time before they celebrated another victory over the Trojans. USC won twenty-six straight over the Beavers until the 2000 season, when Oregon State, led by head coach Dennis Erickson, went 11–1, and beat the Trojans 31–21 along the way.

### 9. WEST VIRGINIA VERSUS PENN STATE

Beginning in the Eisenhower administration, Penn State had command in their rivalry with West Virginia. The Nittany Lions won twenty-five in a row over the Mountaineers from 1959 through 1983. They looked to make it twenty-six in 1994, but West Virginia, led by quarterback Jeff Hostetler (a transfer from—of all places—Penn State), knocked off the Nittany Lions 17–14 in the first-ever night game played at Mountaineer Field.

### 10. MISSOURI VERSUS NEBRASKA

Yes, it's the Cornhuskers again, making their third appearance on this list. Their dominance over Missouri lasted twenty-four seasons, from 1979 through 2002. When Missouri beat Nebraska in 1978, it came a week after the Huskers had beaten number one Oklahoma, and the loss ruined Nebraska's national championship hopes. Nebraska took revenge by beating the Tigers twenty-four years in a row. The games were sometimes close, and none was more fiercely competitive than the 1997 contest decided in overtime (a game that is described in the Hail Mary chapter). Finally, in 2003 Missouri knocked off the Huskers 41–24 at Missouri.

# Monday Night Madness

No one knew for sure how the public would react to NFL games in prime time, let alone on Monday night. But when the NFL and ABC teamed up to put Monday Night Football on the air in 1970, it became a huge success, to the point that it was routinely among the top ten highest rated shows. Through three and a half decades, there have been some memorable Monday nights captured by the ABC crew.

### 1. 2000—NEW YORK JETS 40, MIAMI DOLPHINS 37

The Jets trailed the Dolphins 30–7 early in the fourth quarter, and the capacity crowd at the Meadowlands began to file out. But then the Jets began to show signs of life. Vinny Testaverde hit Laveranues Coles for a touchdown, and the comeback was on. Then, Jermaine Wiggins caught a touchdown pass, and by the time Wayne Chrebet hauled in a 24-yard touchdown pass with a little less than four minutes left, the game was tied. Remarkably, the Dolphins came back on a Jay Fiedler touchdown pass to retake the lead, but the Jets responded once again, as Testaverde hit tackle eligible Jumbo Elliott with a three yard touchdown to force overtime. In the extra session, Jets defensive back Marcus Coleman intercepted two passes. That's right—two. He fumbled away the first one, but his second pick helped set up John Hall for the winning field goal. Since Giants Stadium was home to the original "Miracle at the Meadowlands" in 1978 (when Herman Edwards scored on an unlikely fumble return in the final minute to give the Eagles a win over the Giants), this game was simply dubbed the "Monday Night Miracle."

### 2. 1978—HOUSTON OILERS 35, MIAMI DOLPHINS 30

A November Monday night game at the Astrodome set the stage for the national coming out party for rookie running back Earl Campbell of the Oilers. With a sellout crowd on hand waving light blue pompoms and singing "Luv Ya, Blue," the Oilers and Dolphins faced off in a classic. Bob Griese had a spectacular night for Miami, throwing for 349 yards and two scores, but the game belonged to Campbell. With the Oilers up 28–23 and looking to run out the clock, he took a pitch from quarterback Dan Pastorini and raced 81 yards untouched down the right sideline to ice the game. Campbell finished the game with 199 yards and four touchdowns, and a star was confirmed.

### 3. 1985—MIAMI DOLPHINS 38, CHICAGO BEARS 24

The Bears were 12–0, had just completed back-to-back shut-outs, and looked unbeatable, but in week thirteen they faced the Dolphins—and history. Members of the undefeated 1972 Dolphins team roamed the sidelines, and a raucous Orange Bowl crowd saw Dan Marino put on an aerial show. Miami scored on its first five possessions, including three Marino touchdown passes, to take a 31–10 lead. Steve Fuller, in for the injured Jim McMahon, rallied the Bears with a touchdown, but another Marino touchdown pass clinched it for Miami. It was the only game the Bears lost all season.

### 4. 1994—KANSAS CITY CHIEFS 31, DENVER BRONCOS 28

Two of the NFL's all-time best quarterbacks met each other for the final time in this game, and it was a shootout for the ages. Joe Montana of the Chiefs and Denver's John Elway put on a show befitting two Hall of Famers. The game was close throughout and tied after each quarter. In the fourth quarter Montana drove the Chiefs inside the 5-yard line, where the offense stalled, and Lin Elliott kicked a short field goal for a 24–21 lead. Four minutes remained. After each team turned the ball over, Elway put together one of his patented come-from-behind drives, culminating in a 4-yard touchdown run with a minute and a half left, to put the Broncos up 28–24. But that was a lot of time for Super Joe. Montana completed seven of eight passes on the ensuing drive, including a 5-yarder to Willie Davis to ice the game. It was the highlight of a night that saw Montana throw for 393 yards and three touchdowns.

### 5. 2004—PHILADELPHIA EAGLES 49, DALLAS COWBOYS 21

The eventual NFC champion Eagles gave the Cowboys a good old-fashioned thumping at Texas Stadium behind the arm of Donovan McNabb. But the big story—one that lived on for weeks on cable news and sports radio—occurred before the kickoff. That's when Philadelphia wide receiver Terrell Owens, who's never shy about promoting himself, took part in a pre-taped skit for the opening of *Monday Night Football*. In an obvious cross-promotional ploy, the skit showed Owens in the locker room when actress Nicolette Sheridan from ABC's *Desperate Housewives* appeared, clad only in a towel. Suggestive talk ensued, before she dropped the towel (she's seen only from the rear, and from her back up). No private parts were in view, but the outcry was far and wide. Most felt that at worst it was X-rated, at best it was in poor taste. I agree that it was a poor decision—I would have picked Teri Hatcher if I had to choose one of the Desperate Housewives.

## 6. 1983—GREEN BAY PACKERS 48, WASHINGTON REDSKINS 47

In 1983 the Redskins lost two games all season: Both were played on Monday night, and both were by one point. On an October evening at Lambeau Field, the Skins and the Packers combined for more than 1,000 yards of offense and the most points in Monday Night Football history. Lynn Dickey of the Packers threw for 387 yards and three touchdowns, and he guided Green Bay to the clinching score, a twenty-yard field goal by Jan Stenerud with less than a minute to play. But the Redskins were not done. Joe Theismann led a furious drive that brought Washington inside the 25-yard line with three seconds left, but Mark Moseley missed a 39-yard field goal that would have won the game.

## 7. 2003—DALLAS COWBOYS 35, NEW YORK GIANTS 32

In a week 2 clash at the Meadowlands, the Giants looked to go 2–0, while Bill Parcells was in search of his first win with the underdog Cowboys. Through three quarters Dallas looked to be well on their way to an upset. They had led throughout and had a 29–14 lead. That's when the Giants rallied. A couple of touchdowns brought them even, and when Matt Bryant hit a 30-yard field goal with eleven seconds remaining, the Giants seemingly had won the game. However, Bryant's kickoff squibbed and rolled out of bounds at the 1-yard line—a penalty. The flag gave Dallas the ball at its own 40. On the next play, quarterback Quincy Carter hit Antonio Bryant on a 25-

yard gain, which was notable for two reasons: first, how open Bryant was, and then how easily he was able to get out of bounds to stop the clock. Out came kicker Billy Cundiff, who promptly nailed a 52-yard field goal to tie the game. Cundiff then won it with a 25-yarder in overtime. It was his seventh field goal of the game, tying an NFL record. The game proved to be a turning point for both teams. Dallas went on to a 10–6 record and the playoffs, while the Giants, so close to 2–0, fell apart and finished 4–12.

## 8. 2000—GREEN BAY PACKERS 26, MINNESOTA VIKINGS 20

In a back and forth battle between divisional opponents, the Packers got an overtime miracle to beat the Vikings at rain-soaked Lambeau Field. The Vikings appeared poised to take the game in regulation, but a bad snap on a field goal attempt and an interception thrown by holder Mitch Berger as time expired forced overtime. A little more than three and a half minutes had expired in overtime and the Packers had the ball at the Minnesota 43-yard line. Brett Favre launched a long pass down the sideline in the direction of wide receiver Antonio Freeman, but Freeman slipped, seemingly taking himself out of the play. Viking defensive back Chris Dishman knocked the ball out of the air, where it bounced on the shoulder pad of the unsuspecting Freeman. Freeman cradled it, got up, and scampered into the end zone for the winning score.

## 9. 1982—MINNESOTA VIKINGS 31, DALLAS COWBOYS 27

In the final game of the 1982 regular season at the Metrodome, Tony Dorsett of the Cowboys tied an NFL record when he took a handoff from Danny White and ran 99.5 yards virtually untouched for a score. It was a record-setting night, but it wasn't enough to secure a win. Quarterback Tommy Kramer led the Vikings to the win, clinching a playoff berth for Minnesota.

## 10. 1970—PHILADELPHIA 23, NEW YORK GIANTS 20

It didn't happen often, but this was a night when Howard Cosell was silent. The Eagles hosted the Giants in a late season game. It was bitterly cold in Philadelphia, and the Eagles still played at the University of Pennsylvania's Franklin Field, which had an open-air press box. It was so cold that Keith Jackson bought the warmest coat he could find in the city, but Howard had another remedy for the weather—his trusty flask. How bad could it be to have a few wee nips? By the second quarter, ABC's crew sensed something was off about Cosell. By halftime, Howard was slurring his words so badly that when he tried to pronounce Philadelphia, it sounded something like "Foll-u-dull-fa." During a commercial, Howard was yanked off the air and sent home. Jackson and Dandy Don Meredith covered for him by telling the audience that Howard was not feeling well.

# College Coaches Making The Leap— The Good

Coaching in the NFL is not for someone looking for life-time job security. If you win, you can stick around. But if you lose regularly, you can start looking for other employment. With so much turnaround in coaching, it's not surprising that NFL teams would look to the college ranks for candidates. In the cases of the men below, those teams made wise decisions.

### 1. JIMMY JOHNSON

Johnson came out of the University of Miami where he went 52–9 over five seasons, including a national championship in 1987. He was opinionated and brash, which made him the polar opposite of the legendary Tom Landry, the man he replaced with the Dallas Cowboys before the 1989 season. His team went 1–15 in his first season, but by season three they were in the playoffs. Thanks to a series of successful drafts, the Cowboys were well-stocked for a championship run in Johnson's fourth season. They defeated the 49ers in the NFC Championship Game and the Bills in Super Bowl XXVII, then repeated the feat the next season, which was Johnson's last in Dallas. In his final four years in Dallas, the Cowboys went 50–22.

## 2. JOHN ROBINSON

John Robinson led the USC Trojans for seven seasons, where he won sixty-seven games and was the toast of Los Angeles when he guided USC to the 1978 national championship. He liked L.A. so much that when the Rams needed a coach to replace Ray Malavasi following the 1982 season, he made the trip from the Coliseum to Anaheim Stadium. Robinson's stint with the Rams was largely a success. Behind superstar running back Eric Dickerson, the Rams went to the playoffs in his first four seasons, and six times in his nine years overall. Twice they made the NFC Championship Game: once in 1985, when they lost to the Bears, and again in 1989, when Joe Montana and the 49ers knocked them out of Super Bowl contention.

## 3. TOM COUGHLIN

Coughlin was the head coach for Boston College for three seasons in the early 1990s, and his tenure at Chestnut Hill is best remembered for an upset of then-number-1 Notre Dame in 1993. Before BC, he had been an assistant in the NFL, most recently under Bill Parcells with the Giants. He jumped at the chance to run his own ship with the new franchise in Jacksonville. Coughlin was a stern taskmaster, but it helped him lead his young team to the AFC Championship Game in 1996 (his second year), and to the playoffs in the following three seasons. Coughlin went 68–60 in eight seasons with the Jaguars, and he is currently the head coach of the New York Giants.

## 4. BOBBY ROSS

Bobby Ross spent fifteen seasons on the college sidelines, including 1990, when he guided lightly regarded Georgia Tech of the ACC to a share of the national championship. He was also the head coach at Maryland in 1984, when quarterback Frank Reich helped the Terps complete the greatest comeback in Division 1A history over the Miami Hurricanes. In 1992 the San Diego Chargers put their faith in Ross to replace Dan Henning. He lost his first four games but then won eleven of the last twelve to become the first team to win a division after losing their first four games. Two seasons later, the Chargers upset the Steelers in Pittsburgh to earn their only Super Bowl berth. In nine NFL seasons with San Diego and later Detroit, he finished under .500 only once, and his teams went to the postseason six times. He is the only coach to be named the consensus NCAA coach of the year and also guide a team to the Super Bowl. Ross took on the biggest challenge of his career in 2004, coming out of retirement to resurrect the struggling program at Army.

## 5. DENNIS GREEN

Green coached at two of the toughest universities to recruit for and build a winning program—Northwestern and Stanford—but he earned high marks in both places. At Northwestern, he was named Big Ten Coach of the Year in 1982; and at Stanford, he guided the Cardinal to a win over number one Notre Dame in South Bend. In 1992 he took over the Minnesota Vikings. In ten seasons in Minneapolis, Green took the Vikings to the playoffs eight times and to the NFC Championship Game twice, but both trips were very disappointing: In 1998 the Vikings finished 15–1, but they were upset by Atlanta. In 2000, the Giants pounded the Vikes 41–0 to earn the Super Bowl trip. Green won 101 games with the Vikings, and in 2004 he took over the Arizona Cardinals.

## 6. LOU SABAN

While head coach of Northwestern in the 1950s, Lou Saban was the boss of The Boss. One of his assistant coaches was in fact George Steinbrenner, the man who would go on to own the New York Yankees. After coaching the Wildcats, Saban moved on to Western Illinois University, where his last team went 9–0. Coming off that wildly successful season, he was hired by the Boston Patriots of the AFL to become their first head coach. He went on to coach sixteen seasons in both the AFL and NFL—with the Pats, Bills, Broncos, and again with the Bills (with a one-year stint as head man at the University of Maryland thrown in there). Saban also won two AFL championships in Buffalo and was enshrined in the AFL Hall of Fame.

## 7. BARRY SWITZER

Switzer was one of the most successful coaches in Big 8 Conference history while at Oklahoma, winning 157 games, eight conference championships, and three national championships in his sixteen seasons. However, he was forced out of his job in 1989 amidst numerous scandals. Five years later, with no professional coaching experience, he resurfaced as just the third head coach in the history of the Dallas Cowboys. After owner Jerry Jones had a falling out with Jimmy Johnson over who deserved the credit for the Cowboys' back-to-back Super Bowl championships, Jones hired Switzer, a man very few thought would be successful in the pro game. In his first three seasons in Dallas, Switzer (primarily coaching players brought on during the Johnson era) guided the Cowboys to a 34–14 record, including a win over the Pittsburgh Steelers in Super Bowl XXX. He was fired after posting a 6–10 record in his fourth year in Big D.

## 8. DON CORYELL

Don Coryell was one of the brightest offensive minds to ever man the sidelines. He first came to national attention at San Diego State, where he compiled a record of 104–19–2, had two unbeaten and untied seasons, posted winning streaks of twenty-five and thirty-one games, and won three bowl games. In 1973 he took over the St. Louis Cardinals and led the Redbirds to their most successful three-season run during their tenure in St. Louis. Between 1973 and 1975, Coryell's team won thirty-one games. No Cardinal team since 1975 has won in double digits for a season. Coryell coached fourteen seasons in the NFL with the Cardinals and Chargers, won five division titles, and twice took his team to within one game of the Super Bowl. He is the only coach to win 100 games in both college and the pros.

## 9. DICK VERMEIL

Dick Vermeil coached only two seasons at UCLA, but he capped them off famously, guiding his Bruins to an upset over number 1 Ohio State in the 1976 Rose Bowl. That was enough to convince the Philadelphia Eagles to give him the responsibility of turning their franchise around. By his third season, the Eagles were in the playoffs, where they dropped a heartbreaking 14–13 decision to the Falcons in the first-ever wild card playoff game. They made the playoffs in their next three seasons, including the Eagles' first-ever trip to the Super Bowl following the 1980 season. After a disappointing 1982 season, Vermeil cited burnout as his reason for stepping down. He did not appear on an NFL sideline for another fifteen seasons, when he took over for the Rams. After three years and a Super Bowl championship in St. Louis, Vermeil took a year off and then became the coach of the Kansas City Chiefs.

## 10. BILL WALSH

A coach with a record of 17–7 in two seasons at Stanford could hardly be expected to become one of the greatest coaches and innovators in NFL history, but Bill Walsh did just that. Three years after taking over the moribund 49ers, he led them to a win in Super Bowl XVI. Eight seasons later, he led San Francisco to victory in Super Bowl XXIII and retired with a record of 102–63–1.

# College Coaches Making The Leap— The Bad

As we see from the list below, it's a big jump from the life of recruiting, fundraising, and schmoozing with alumni and boosters to the NFL. Here are ten men who should have stayed in school.

## 1. STEVE SPURRIER

Steve Spurrier's record as head coach at his alma mater, Florida, speaks for itself. In twelve seasons he won 122 games and celebrated the 1996 national championship with a win over rival Florida State. His teams won at least nine games every year and his .861 winning percentage in conference games is the best ever. Following the 2001 season, he resigned from Florida and shortly thereafter was given a huge contract to become head coach of the Washington Redskins. But the self-described "old ball coach" discovered that in the NFL, his fun and gun offense was not going up against the Ole Miss defense every week. After a 7–9 season, he began to lose control of the team. When his second year was even worse, (5–11), he handed in his resignation to owner Daniel Snyder. Spurrier took over the program at the University of South Carolina in 2005.

## 2. **MIKE RILEY**

Despite only two seasons as head coach at Oregon State, in which he compiled a record of just 8–14, Mike Riley had built up a reputation as a coach who could put together an offense. That was enough for the San Diego Chargers, who brought Riley in for the 1999 season. Unfortunately, the team was in disarray, fractured by the Ryan Leaf draft fiasco from the previous season. Riley went 8–8 in his first year, but the team slipped to 1–15 and 5–11, and he was let go after losing his last nine games. In 2003 Riley returned to Corvallis and took his former job at Oregon State.

## 3. **LOU HOLTZ**

Lou Holtz had a great run at North Carolina State, winning four straight bowl games. Later on he'd win a national championship with Notre Dame. But, in 1976, he made probably the worst decision of his career: accepting the New York Jets head coaching position. Holtz thought his rah-rah college temperament would work in the pro game, even penning a fight song (!) that he tried to get the team to sing. Not surprisingly, the team floundered, losing ten of its first thirteen games, and Holtz quit with one game left on the schedule.

## 4. **BILL PETERSON**

Following a successful eleven-season stay at Florida State, Peterson spent a year at Rice University in Houston. Shortly thereafter, the hometown Oilers were looking to fill their head coach position. His run under the bright lights of the Astrodome was short and not so sweet. His 1972 team went just

1–13, and after losing the first five games in 1973, Peterson was let go. Despite such a bad pro record, he did have an eye for coaching talent. Some of the men he employed as assistants included Bill Parcells, Joe Gibbs, Don James, and Earl Bruce.

### 5. DENNIS ERICKSON

Dennis Erickson is best compared to a baseball prospect who tears up Triple–A pitching but can't hit the curve ball when he gets to the big leagues. Erickson had a fantastic career as a college coach: He won 113 games in thirteen seasons at Idaho, Wyoming, Washington State, and Miami, including two national championships with the Hurricanes. In 1995 the Seattle Seahawks named him head coach, and his four year record was spotty: 31–33 with no playoff appearances. Not terrible, but not good enough for the Seahawks, who fired him and hired Mike Holmgren away from the Green Bay Packers. Erickson went back to the college ranks, where he coached Oregon State to a BCS bowl. In 2003 he returned to the pros, where he had a difficult two-season stint with the woeful San Francisco 49ers.

### 6. CHUCK FAIRBANKS

Chuck Fairbanks's six-year reign as head coach of the New England Patriots was not terrible. In fact, he went to the play-offs twice: once in 1976, and once in his final season, 1978. The former coach of Oklahoma University, Fairbanks won forty-six games for the Patriots, but shortly before the 1978 season finale against the Dolphins in the Orange Bowl, the rumor mill was abuzz that Fairbanks was about to sign a contract to coach the University of Colorado. Fairbanks was miffed that the club's owners, the Sullivan family, were getting a little too hands-on. Billy Sullivan suspended Fairbanks for the game, but he was reinstated for the team's playoff game, a 31–14 loss to the Oilers. Fairbanks took the brunt of the criticism for the defeat, and left for Colorado shortly thereafter.

### 7. DICK MacPHERSON
A likable guy who inspired passion in his players, MacPherson left Syracuse University in 1991 to join the Patriots, who were coming off a dismal 1–15 season. A 6–10 record in his first year raised expectations, but New England regressed in MacPherson's second year, sliding to 2–14. MacPherson also battled health problems that season, missing time with diverticulitis. He was let go and replaced by Bill Parcells.

### 8. RICH BROOKS
If ever one man seemed the right fit for a job, it was Rich Brooks at the University of Oregon. He guided the Ducks for eighteen years, and in the final six years he went to four bowl games, including a Rose Bowl appearance versus Penn State in his final campaign, 1994. That was the first time in close to four decades that the Ducks spent their postseason in Pasadena. But the lure of the NFL took Brooks away from Oregon and the PAC 10, and he was hired to coach the Rams in their first season in St. Louis. Things started out great: The Rams were 5–1 and looked like they could become a surprise playoff team. But they went 2–8 the rest of the way, then 6–10 the next season, and Brooks was sent packing. The Rams hired Dick Vermeil as a replacement, and within three years they were Super Bowl champs. Brooks, as of this writing, is the head coach at the University of Kentucky.

### 9. DARRYL ROGERS
Darryl Rogers spent twenty years on the collegiate sideline, including stops at Michigan State and Arizona State. It was

from the latter that he was recruited by the Detroit Lions to take over in 1985. The Lions struggled his first year, finishing 7–9, but any hope that they would build from that was quickly dismissed, as the team went just 11–31 over the next three seasons. Rogers was dismissed eleven games into the 1988 season.

### 10. BUTCH DAVIS

Butch Davis was a former assistant coach under Jimmy Johnson, so most thought it was a great hire when he was brought in to the University of Miami to restore their reputation. In 2000 he led the Hurricanes to a BCS bowl and a number 2 national ranking, setting the Canes up for their run to the national title the next year. But Davis would not be there. He was hired by the Cleveland Browns to take over for Chris Palmer. He went 7–9 in his first season, and earned a wild card berth his second year, but the Browns collapsed in 2003. Davis resigned midway through the 2004 season, finishing with an overall regular season of 24–35 in his three-plus seasons in Cleveland.

# Back To School

They say the best years of your life are spent in college. For some men, the harsh realities of the NFL coaching life have them yearning for better days. And that sends them back to school— to become college coaches.

## 1. AL GROH

Coaching under Bill Parcells for close to two decades with the New York Giants, New England Patriots, and New York Jets gave Al Groh a reputation as one of the top linebacker coaches in the game. When Parcells stepped down as coach of the Jets following the 1999 season, and defensive coordinator Bill Belichick turned the head coaching job down, the Jets turned to Groh. Like Parcells, Groh was tough on his players, and from the beginning things looked good: The Jets started 4–0 and had a 9–4 record, but they lost out on a playoff spot by losing their final three games. In the off-season, Groh was contacted by his alma mater, the University of Virginia, about its vacant coaching position. He accepted, and led the Cavaliers to three bowl games in his first four years in Charlottesville.

## 2. **PETE CARROLL**

Pete Carroll was a four-year head coach in the NFL, compiling a 33–31 record with the Jets (for one year) and the Patriots (for three). But Carroll was criticized for being soft and too much of a so-called player's coach. That may not have worked for Carroll in the NFL, but it sure has worked for him in college. He discovered that upon being named coach at USC in 2001. In his first four seasons on the sidelines of the Coliseum, his teams went to bowl games each season, including three BCS bowls. He coached two Heisman Trophy winners, and he won two national championships to bring the Trojans back to national prominence.

## 3. **BILL CALLAHAN**

In January 2003 he was coaching the Oakland Raiders in the Super Bowl. Twelve months later, he was out of a job. Such was life for Bill Callahan working under Al Davis, but Callahan was not out of work for long. In a surprise move, he was hired by the University of Nebraska to take over for Frank Solich, who was fired in 2003 despite a 9–3 record. Callahan announced plans to employ a pass-oriented West Coast offense, a monumental change for the usually smashmouth offense of the legendary Tom Osborne. After one season, the jury was still out on Callahan, as the Cornhuskers finished just 5–6. It was their first season without a bowl appearance since 1961.

## 4. **BILL WALSH**

When he retired from the San Francisco 49ers following Super Bowl XXIII, there was a good bit of speculation as to whether Bill Walsh would ever take another NFL job. The answer was no, but he did come back to coach again—in 1992, at Stanford. Walsh had spent two years with the Cardinal in the 1970s before he coached the 49ers. His first year back was a smashing success: ten wins, a top-ten finish, and a Blockbuster Bowl win over Penn State. But things went south after that. Following seasons of 4–7 and 3–7–1, Walsh stepped down.

## 5. DAN HENNING

A man with a reputation as a brilliant offensive coach, Dan Henning had limited success as an NFL head coach. His record with San Diego and Atlanta was just 38–73–1. Despite that, Boston College tapped Henning in 1994 when Tom Coughlin left for the Jacksonville Jaguars. Henning fared well in his first season, capping a seven-win campaign with an upset win over Kansas State in the Aloha Bowl. But soon the program became embroiled in scandal, and Henning was removed from the job after three years and a 16–19–1 record.

## 6. JUNE JONES

After three years that are mostly remembered for a heated sideline argument with quarterback Jeff George, Atlanta Falcons coach June Jones went back to the scholastic ranks to take over the program at his alma mater, the University of Hawaii. In his first six seasons he guided the Warriors to a 49–30 record, including two wins in three bowl appearances.

## 7. GENE STALLINGS

The one-time Texas A&M coach had a rough go in the NFL, struggling to a 23–34–1 record with the Arizona Cardinals (but, really, who doesn't struggle with the Cardinals?). In 1990 he was hired for one of the most prestigious college jobs at Alabama. He quickly returned the Crimson Tide to prominence, accumulating a 70–16–1 mark. No win was bigger than the Sugar Bowl following the 1992 season, when Alabama knocked off the Miami Hurricanes 34–13 to win the national championship.

## 8. **SAM RUTIGLIANO**

Sam Rutigliano was a spirited Brooklyn native who guided the Cleveland Browns for seven seasons, including the magical "Cardiac Kids" season of 1980, when the Browns won twelve games and the AFC Central. Five years after he was let go, he resurfaced with Division 1AA Liberty University. He spent eleven years with the Flyers, compiling a 67–53 record, which makes him the all-time winningest coach in Liberty history.

## 9. **JOHN MACKOVIC**

John Mackovic was something of a wunderkind when he was hired by the Kansas City Chiefs in 1983 at the age of forty, but his four-year record at Arrowhead Stadium was just 30–34, and he made just one playoff appearance. However, the University of Illinois was impressed with Mackovic, and he went 30–16–1 with bowl appearances in each of his four years in Champaign. That got him the job at Texas, where he went 41–28–2 in seven often tumultuous seasons in Austin. His 1998 team won the inaugural Big 12 Championship Game over defending national champion Nebraska, but his fate was sealed the following season when his team was thumped 66–3 by UCLA. That loss led to his dismissal at season's end. He later resurfaced at Arizona, but a near revolt by players and a poor won-loss record prompted the school to release him following the 2003 season.

## 10. **DAVE WANNSTEDT**

The defensive coordinator for the 1992 Super Bowl champion Dallas Cowboys, Wannstedt left Big D to take on the unenviable task of replacing Mike Ditka in Chicago. He did not have near the success of Iron Mike in the Windy City, going 41–57 in six seasons, with only one playoff win. Later, he replaced Jimmy Johnson with the Dolphins where he won—but not enough. Despite making the playoffs in his first two years, the Fish never got to the conference championship game. He stepped down during a disastrous 2004 season, after which he was named head coach at his alma mater, Pitt.

# Going Bowling At Different Schools

Some coaches love the college game so much they like to spread themselves around to different universities. The following men have each led at least three different schools to postseason bowl games.

### 1. LOU HOLTZ

At the age of 33, Holtz led William & Mary to the Tangerine Bowl, where they lost to Toledo. It would be the first of five schools he would guide to bowl appearances. Holtz got his first bowl victory when he led North Carolina State to a 49–13 win over West Virginia (coached by Bobby Bowden), and he would take the Wolfpack to three more bowls before moving on to the University of Arkansas. He coached the Razorbacks to six bowl appearances, the most noteworthy a 31–6 upset over Oklahoma in the 1978 Orange Bowl. Later on he guided Notre Dame to nine bowls, including a 1989 Fiesta Bowl win over West Virginia that gave the Irish the national championship. Following his era at South Bend, he moved on to South Carolina and guided the Gamecocks to back-to-back Outback Bowl wins over Ohio State.

## 2. EARL BRUCE

Earl Bruce was best known as the man who replaced Woody Hayes at Ohio State. He guided the Buckeyes to eight bowl appearances, but he lost both times he took OSU to the Rose Bowl. Before Columbus, he had been to bowls with two other schools: Tampa, who he coached to the 1972 Tangerine Bowl, and Iowa State, who he took to two bowls in the late 1970s. Following his dismissal from Ohio State, he had a brief, turbulent reign at Colorado State, during which he led them to a win over Oregon in the 1990 Freedom Bowl.

## 3. BILL MALLORY

The 38-year-old Mallory led Miami (Ohio), his alma mater, to the Tangerine Bowl in 1973, where they knocked off Florida. After that, he led three more schools to bowl success. First, at Colorado, he led the Buffaloes to two bowl appearances, including the 1977 Orange Bowl following a surprise Big 8 championship. In 1983, he coached Northern Illinois to a win over Cal State Fullerton in the California Bowl. From that point, he guided Indiana to six bowl games between 1986 and 1993.

## 4. LARRY SMITH

Another coach who led four schools to bowl games was Larry Smith. He got his first taste of bowl life in 1979, when his Tulane team lost the Liberty Bowl to Joe Paterno and Penn State. Later he moved on to Arizona, where his Wildcats went to consecutive bowls in 1985 and 1986. In a controversial switch, he left for PAC 10 rival USC, whom he coached to five bowls, including three straight Rose Bowls. The final stop on his bowl journey was at Missouri, where in 1997 and 1998 the Tigers played in the Holiday Bowl and the Insight.com Bowl.

## 5. DENNIS FRANCHIONE

Franchione is unique among the coaches above him on this list in that he went to bowl games with four different schools, but he did it within a short eight-year span. In 1997 he went to the Insight.com Bowl with New Mexico, where the Lobos lost to Arizona. Soon after, he was named coach at Texas Christian University, and guided the Horned Frogs to consecutive bowls in 1998 and 1999. After TCU, he went south to the storied program at Alabama, and though his time there was short lived, he did guide them to the Independence Bowl in 2001. Three years later, he was back in a bowl game with Texas A&M, with a Cotton Bowl loss to Tennessee.

## 6. BEAR BRYANT

The legend who coached Alabama to twenty-four bowl games also went bowling at two other schools. Bryant went 3–1 in four bowls at the University of Kentucky, before losing his only bowl game at Texas A&M. With Alabama, he was 7–1 in the Sugar Bowl, 2–3 in the Orange Bowl, 1–3 in the Cotton Bowl, and 2–2 in the Liberty Bowl. His career bowl record was 15–12–2.

## 7. MACK BROWN

Best known around the rest of America as the coach at Texas and the man who can't beat Oklahoma, Brown guided the Longhorns to seven consecutive bowls through the 2004 season. In addition to that is a dramatic 37–35 win over Michigan in the January 2005 Rose Bowl and the explosive 41–38 win in the 2006 national championship over Southern California—the first for the Longhorns in thirty-five years. Before he took over in Austin, Brown was the coach at North Carolina where he went to five

TEXAS A&M MEDIA RELATIONS OFFICE

Dennis Franchione took four different teams to bown gamews over just eight season, including Texas A&M.

consecutive bowls with the Tar Heels. Previously, he had coached Tulane to the 1987 Independence Bowl.

### 8. JACKIE SHERILL
Sherill took over the Pittsburgh program the season after Johnny Majors guided the Panthers to a national champion- ship in 1977. He guided the Panthers to five bowl games, including a win over Georgia in the 1982 Sugar Bowl. He had some help from his quarterback in that game—a fellow named Dan Marino. Moving on from Pitt, Sherill arrived in College Station, Texas, and brought his Texas A&M Aggies to three straight Cotton Bowls. Through the 1990s, Sherill coached at Mississippi State, appearing in six bowls, but winning just two.

### 9. JOHNNY MAJORS
After coaching Iowa State to two bowl appearances in the early 1970s, Johnny Majors entered the national spotlight at Pitt, thanks to a fleet running back named Tony Dorsett. Pitt won the national championship with a 27–3 thumping of Georgia in the 1977 Sugar Bowl. Soon after, Majors was named head coach at his alma mater, Tennessee, where he won seven of his eleven bowl appearances between 1979 and 1992.

### 10. JOHN L. SMITH
Before John L. Smith got the head coaching job at Michigan State—a team he led to the Alamo Bowl in 2003—he coached at two non-BCS schools. He took Utah State to the Humani- tarian Bowl in 1997, then he guided Louisville to a 1–4 record in five bowl appearances.

# Bowl Blowouts

Every year the college bowl season comes and fans hope for one thing: close, memorable games. But that doesn't always happen. Here are some of the worst mismatches in bowl history, in chronological order.

### 1. 1902 ROSE BOWL—MICHIGAN 49, STANFORD 0
One of the biggest blowouts in bowl history came in the very first Rose Bowl game. Fielding Yost's Michigan Wolverines capped off an 11–0 season, in which they outscored opponents 555–0 (really!), with a 49–0 thumping of Stanford. Neil Snow scored five touchdowns out of the backfield for Michigan in the game, which was played at Tournament Park, since the Rose Bowl had yet to be built.

### 2. 1948 ROSE BOWL—MICHIGAN 49, USC 0
Different field, different legendary coach, but the same bowl and the same result. Michigan finished off a perfect season under coach Fritz Crisler by blasting Southern California. Jack Weisenburger had three touchdowns for the Wolverines, whose defense allowed the Trojans past midfield only twice in the entire game.

### 3. 1953 ORANGE BOWL—ALABAMA 61, SYRACUSE 6

The first nationally televised Orange Bowl turned into a rout, as the Crimson Tide of Alabama, a heavy favorite, trounced the Syracuse Orangemen 61–6. The Tide ran up almost 600 yards of offense and scored fifty-four unanswered points over the final three quarters. Alabama's Bobby Luna and Tommy Lewis both scored two touchdowns, and Luna converted seven PATs. Alabama's final score was a touchdown reception by Joe Cummings, who caught a 22-yard pass from backup quarterback Bart Starr.

### 4. 1973 ORANGE BOWL—NEBRASKA 40, NOTRE DAME 6

Johnny Rodgers of Nebraska capped off his Heisman Trophy winning career with a monster effort in the Cornhusker's whipping of the Fighting Irish. In what was also Nebraska head coach Bob Devaney's career swan song, Rodgers ran for three scores, threw a 32-yard pass to Frosty Anderson for another, then hauled in a 50-yard pass from David Humm for a fifth score. All that came in the first three quarters. Notre Dame could only muster a late touchdown to avert a shutout.

### 5. 1984 ROSE BOWL—UCLA 45, ILLINOIS 9

The Fighting Illini were flying high as they ventured west to Pasadena for the Rose Bowl. They held a 10–1 record and looked to add to it at the expense of 6–4–1 UCLA. But the Bruins, playing on their home field, took it to Illinois, as Rick Neuheisel (future coach of Washington and Colorado) threw four touchdown passes, two of those to wideout Karl Dorrell (future coach of UCLA).

### 6. 1988 HOLIDAY BOWL—OKLAHOMA STATE 62, WYOMING 14

It was the Barry Sanders Show as the Heisman winner ran over the Wyoming defense for 222 yards and five touchdowns, despite only playing the first three quarters. Oklahoma State quarterback Mike Gundy had a remarkably accurate game, going twenty for twenty-four and 315 yards and a pair of touchdowns. Wyoming's 14 points were the fewest in a Holiday Bowl game to that point.

### 7. 1990 HOLIDAY BOWL—TEXAS A&M 65, BRIGHAM YOUNG 14

For the second time in three years, the Heisman Trophy winner came to San Diego for the Holiday Bowl. But this time, the winner did not fare as well. BYU quarterback Ty Detmer, who took home the trophy just a few weeks earlier, was knocked out of the game in the second half. By that time, the Aggies had run up a 37–7 lead. Detmer's opposition, A&M's Bucky Richardson, was the big star of the game. Richardson threw for 203 yards and a touchdown. He also ran in two scores and added another on a reception from Darren Lewis on a halfback option play.

### 8. 1996 FIESTA BOWL—NEBRASKA 62, FLORIDA 24

Nebraska won its second straight undisputed national championship with a 38-point ambush of Florida in the Fiesta Bowl. The Cornhuskers embarrassed the Gators defense by amassing 629 yards of offense, including 524 (!) on the ground. Tommy Frazier set a Fiesta Bowl record with 199 yards on the ground, while Lawrence Phillips chipped in with 165 yards and three touchdowns. Trailing 10–6 after one period, the Cornhuskers scored 29 points in the second and never looked back. The 62 points were a Fiesta Bowl record and a Nebraska record for points in a bowl game, at least until . . .

### 9. 2000 ALAMO BOWL—NEBRASKA 66, NORTHWESTERN 17

The Cornhuskers, off (for them) a disappointing 9–2 season,

spotted the Wildcats a 10–7 lead early in the second quarter before exploding for 31 points before the break. Dan Alexander ran for a Nebraska bowl record 240 yards and two touchdowns, and Eric Crouch ran for two scores and passed for two more, both to wideout Matt Davison. The overmatched Wildcats could muster only a 69-yard touchdown run by Damien Anderson over the final three quarters.

### 10. 2005 ORANGE BOWL—USC 55, OKLAHOMA 19

USC won its second straight national championship, thumping the Sooners behind Heisman Trophy-winner Matt Leinart, who tossed a record five touchdown passes. The Trojans broke the game open in the final twenty minutes of the first half, scoring 38 points, and putting the game completely out of reach. USC's Steve Smith had three touchdown receptions to set an Orange Bowl record. It was the third straight year the Trojans won a BCS bowl game, having defeated Iowa in the Orange Bowl in 2003 and Michigan in the 2004 Rose Bowl.

# The "What" Bowl?

College bowl choices are always so delicious and tempting: Orange, Peach, Sugar, Rose, Fiesta. These are the bowl games we're accustomed to every year. But there are smaller bowls that don't get enough recognition and some that came and went with little fanfare. Here are ten long-forgotten bowl games.

### 1. BACARDI BOWL
The Bacardi Bowl was played just one time in (where else?) the Caribbean. At the end of the 1937 season, Auburn took on Villanova in Havana, Cuba. The offenses of the two teams must have been enjoying some of Havana's legendary nightlife because they certainly didn't come to play. The game ended in a 7–7 slugfest, in what is surely the only college postseason game that will be played on the island of Cuba.

### 2. BLUEGRASS BOWL
As one would suspect, the one and only Bluegrass Bowl took place in the state of Kentucky. Louisville hosted the December 1958 game between Oklahoma State and Florida State. The Cowboys took the game 15–6 and finished the season number 19 in the AP poll.

### 3. DIXIE BOWL

Legion Field in Birmingham, Alabama was the site of the Dixie Bowl, which was played twice, following the 1948 and 1949 seasons. Arkansas won the inaugural game, a 21–19 conquest of William & Mary, while Baylor was victorious in the final game, 20–7 over Wake Forest.

### 4. AVIATION BOWL

What better city for a game called the Aviation Bowl than the birthplace of the Wright Brothers and the home of the Air Force Museum? Dayton, Ohio was the host city for the only Aviation Bowl following the 1961 season. New Mexico knocked off Western Michigan 28–12.

### 5. SALAD BOWL

Yes, there really was a postseason "classic" called the Salad Bowl. It was played five consecutive seasons from 1948 through 1952 in Arizona, and in an effort to boost local interest, Arizona or Arizona State took part in three of the games. The home cooking didn't help, though, as the schools went 0–3.

### 6. OIL BOWL

Would it surprise you that a game called the Oil Bowl was played in the great state of Texas? Houston hosted the game in 1946 and 1947, and both games were won by teams from Georgia. In 1946 Georgia beat Tulsa 20–6, and the next year saw Georgia Tech knock off St. Mary's 41–19. Houston later hosted two other bowls, the Bluebonnet Bowl, which was played from 1959 through 1987, and the Ev1.net (a.k.a. Houston) Bowl, which has been played since 2000.

### 7. GOTHAM BOWL

In 1961 and 1962 New York City got into the postseason act with the Gotham Bowl, played at Yankee Stadium. The first year, Baylor beat Washington State 24–9 (those are wins in two obscure bowl games for the Bears) and in the second, Nebraska beat Miami (Florida) 36–34 in the first of five bowl meetings between those two schools. The other four meetings (three times in the Orange Bowl and once in the Rose Bowl) all had national championship implications.

### 8. FORT WORTH CLASSIC

In 1921 the first and only Fort Worth Classic saw Centre dismantle Texas Christian University 63–7. When the host school loses by eight touchdowns, there's usually not much need to stage another contest.

### 9. CHERRY BOWL

Don't associate cherries with Pontiac, Michigan? Well, the Cherry Bowl was held there twice, following the 1984 and 1985 seasons. In 1984 Army knocked off Michigan State 10–6, the last time the Cadets won a bowl game. Then in 1985 Maryland blasted Syracuse 35–18.

### 10. RAISIN BOWL

From 1945 through 1949, Fresno, California hosted the Raisin Bowl five times. San Jose State won two of the games. The other three were won by the football powerhouses of Occidental, Drake, and Pacific.

# BCS (And Pre-BCS) BS

It's a question college football fans, administrators, media, and coaches ask every year: Who is really number one? Unlike all other college sports, college football's division 1A championship is not decided on the field. It's been decided for years based on polls conducted by coaches (who probably have not seen 80 percent of the other teams play) and media. Back in the 1990s, after years of watching the best teams not play each other on bowl day because of the bowl setup, the NCAA adopted the BCS (Bowl Coalition Series), which was created to get the top two teams in the country to face off to decide a national champion. The NCAA implemented this system by using coaches, media polls, and computer rankings to choose the top two teams. But it's not always that easy. Here are ten instances where there was a question of who should be playing for the national championship, both before and after the advent of the BCS.

## 1. 2004: USC, OKLAHOMA, AUBURN

The BCS is supposed to bring together the top two teams in the country to take part in a championship game. But what happens when you have three schools (four if you count Utah from the Mountain West), all from major conferences, who are undefeated? That's precisely what happened in 2004 when USC from the PAC 10, Oklahoma out of the Big 12, and the SEC's Auburn all finished the regular season unbeaten and untied. The final BCS rankings placed the Trojans and Sooners in the championship game, leaving the Tigers out of the mix. Auburn was placed in the Sugar Bowl to play a two-loss Virginia Tech team, winners of the ACC. Auburn won their game to finish unbeaten, then watched USC dismantle Oklahoma to win the national championship.

## 2. **2003: LSU, OKLAHOMA, USC**

One year before USC won the BCS Championship, they were involved in another BCS controversy. In 2003 the Trojans, who had lost just one game all season, a triple overtime heartbreaker at Cal, went into bowl season as the number 1 team in both the ESPN/USA Today Coaches poll and the Associated Press media poll. However, computer rankings had both the Tigers and Sooners above the Trojans, and USC—despite being number 1 in the rankings—was left out of the BCS Championship Game. This left an intriguing possibility open: Since USC was atop the Associated Press poll, and the AP writers were not compelled to vote for the winner of the BCS Championship Game as national champion, could the Trojans claim a share of the title with a Rose Bowl win over Michigan? USC took care of business with a comfortable win over the Wolverines in Pasadena, then watched as LSU knocked off Oklahoma 21–14 in the Sugar Bowl. The final result? LSU was the BCS champion, while AP voters stayed with USC. it was the first time in the history of the Bowl Coalition Series that two teams shared the national championship.

### 3. 2001: NEBRASKA, COLORADO, OREGON

In 2001 the battle for the national championship came down to who would face off against undefeated Miami (Fla.) at the Rose Bowl. Nebraska was undefeated through their first eleven games, with only a road game against Colorado on Thanksgiving weekend standing between them and the Hurricanes. But the Buffaloes trounced the Cornhuskers 62–36, knocking Nebraska down in the polls and out of the Big 12 title game. Two other Big 12 teams had a chance to step up and claim a spot in the championship game, but Oklahoma lost to Oklahoma State, and then Texas lost to Colorado in the Big 12 title game. A loss by Tennessee knocked the Volunteers out of contention, leaving only three teams with claims: 10–2 Colorado, the Big 12 champ, 11–1 Oregon, the PAC 10 champ, and Nebraska. In a surprise, Nebraska was chosen, leaving both the Ducks and Buffaloes scratching their heads. The chorus of complaint only grew louder when Miami walloped Nebraska 38–14. Oregon had to settle for a Fiesta Bowl win over Colorado and a final number 2 national ranking.

### 4. 2000: FLORIDA STATE, MIAMI

When two schools share identical records, but one of those schools beat the other head-to-head, shouldn't the team that won that game have the higher ranking? You would think so, but don't tell that to fans of the Miami Hurricanes. In 2000 the Seminoles were undefeated and entered the Orange Bowl to take on their old nemeses, Miami. The only blemish on the young Hurricanes' record was an early season loss at the University of Washington. Miami hung on in a tight contest for the win, and both teams won throughout the regular season. With unbeaten Oklahoma waiting in the BCS championship game, the final BCS standings had Oklahoma number 1, Florida State number 2, and Miami number 3. Hurricanes supporters and the national media howled, but to no avail. Oklahoma would beat a listless Florida State team 13–2 to win the championship, a game during which Bobby Bowden questioned a national television audience whether his team really belonged in the game.

### 5. 1994: NEBRASKA, PENN STATE

The last big controversy before the advent of the BCS came in 1994 when both Nebraska and Penn State went through the regular season undefeated. Penn State had actually been number 1 early in the season, but after a 35–29 win over Indiana (a game not nearly as close as the final score indicates, due to Penn State giving up two very late touchdowns with their second string defense on the field), the Nittany Lions fell to number 2. Nebraska moved up to number 1, beat a good Colorado team near the end of the regular season, then beat Miami on their home field in the Orange Bowl to finish 13–0. Penn State, led by two top-five NFL draft picks in Ki-Jana Carter and Kerry Collins, won the Big Ten, then beat an overmatched Oregon team in the Rose Bowl for a 12–0 season. Sometimes, with two national powers in a situation like this, a split poll crowns two national champions, but not this time. Nebraska emerged on top of both the writers and coaches polls, the first championship for coach Tom Osborne.

### 6. 1990: VIRGINIA, GEORGIA TECH, COLORADO

1990 was the year after which college football really needed to take a look at how it chose teams for bowls and crowned national champions. Through the first half of that year, Virginia was the feel-good story of college football. The Cavaliers, led by Shawn Moore and Herman Moore, had a 7–0 record entering a home contest with Georgia Tech. As the number 1 team in the country, Virginia was drawing interest from the major bowls, and they, in fact, had already agreed to play in the Sugar Bowl. But there was a lot of college football left to be played. First, the Yellow Jackets, who had a tie with North Carolina as the only blemish on their record, beat Virginia 41–38. Virginia lost three more regular season games but were still locked into the Sugar Bowl, where they lost to Tennessee. Georgia Tech, meanwhile, did not lose again, but because they were from the ACC and did not have a commitment from a major bowl, they ended up in the Citrus Bowl, where they beat Nebraska. But even that was not enough to win an undisputed national championship. The Yellow Jackets split the title with Colorado, who had a loss and a tie early in the season. They also had a win that should have been a loss, when they were given five downs to score near the goal line in a regular season game at Missouri.

## 7. 1993: FLORIDA STATE

Bobby Bowden was still looking for his first national championship when he took his top-ranked, undefeated Seminoles into South Bend to take on Notre Dame's undefeated Fighting Irish. When Florida State lost 24–17, it looked like Bowden's national title hopes were history. But the following week, Notre Dame lost to Boston College, knocking them out of the number 1 slot, and the Seminoles were ready to jump back in. They beat Nebraska 18–16 in the Orange Bowl, while Notre Dame beat Texas A&M 24–21 in the Cotton Bowl. When the final rankings came out, Florida State was crowned national champion despite their head-to-head loss to the Irish.

FSU SPORTS INFORMATION

Florida State's Bobby Bowden won his first national
championship at the expense of Notre Dame, a team that beat
FSU in the regular season.

### 8. 1969: TEXAS, PENN STATE

Texas cemented its claim to a national championship with a 21–17 Cotton Bowl win over Notre Dame, but the real national championship was won with their 15–14 win over number 2 Arkansas just a few weeks before. President Nixon, who was at the game, even, proclaimed the Longhorns champions following that contest. The only problem was that Penn State was also undefeated, and they went on to win the Orange Bowl over Missouri. It would have looked pretty bad had Texas stumbled against Notre Dame and Penn State had won, but the Longhorns kept up their side of the bargain and few (outside of Happy Valley) could complain.

### 9. 1964: ALABAMA, ARKANSAS

Think the rankings were screwy when they were based on bowl results? Then how about crowning a champion before the bowls were even played? That's the way it was done until the mid 1960s, but 1964 was a catalyst for change. Alabama finished the regular season undefeated, as did Arkansas, who ended their campaign with a big 14–13 win over nationally ranked Texas—the same Texas team who would beat Alabama in the Orange Bowl. Meanwhile, the Razorbacks took care of Nebraska in the Cotton Bowl. But because the bowls didn't count in the voting, one-loss Alabama finished number 1 and unbeaten Arkansas was number 2.

### 10. 1978: ALABAMA, USC

Much like what happened to Florida State in 1993, Alabama suffered an early season loss to USC but was able to recover to share the national championship with those same Trojans. USC's 24–14 win over Alabama propelled them in the polls, and they were crowned the UPI national champion after a 17–10 Rose Bowl win over Michigan. But Alabama had one advantage over the Trojans heading into the Sugar Bowl: They had the opportunity to play undefeated and number 1 Penn State. By virtue of their 14–7 win over the Nittany Lions, the Crimson Tide had the most votes in the final AP poll, splitting the national championship.

# When Bad Losses Happen To Good Teams

Even the best teams can have a bad day. After all, there is merit to the expression that begins, "On any given Sunday." But sometimes a great team suffers such a shocking loss that the entire country takes notice. Here are some of the memorable "bad" losses.

### 1. 1964 BALTIMORE COLTS

Behind the arm of John Unitas and the brilliant coaching of young Don Shula, the 12–2 Colts headed into the NFL Championship Game in Cleveland as a big favorite over the Browns. In addition to Unitas, the Colts were loaded with stars like Lenny Moore, Raymond Berry, Gino Marchetti, John Mackey, and Tom Matte. True, the Browns had Jim Brown, but in this game it was the Browns' defense, with which it pitched an improbable shutout, and journeyman quarterback Frank Ryan, who threw three touchdowns to Gary Collins, that spearheaded Cleveland's 27–0 upset. It was the first championship for head coach Blanton Collier, the man who replaced the legendary Paul Brown, and the Browns' young owner, Art Modell.

### 2. 1970 DALLAS COWBOYS

The Cowboys suffered perhaps their most humiliating defeat under Tom Landry when the Cardinals came to Dallas for a week nine Monday Night Football encounter. The Cowboys, despite having been a perennial playoff team, were still battling the stigma of being unable to "win the big game." But on this night Dallas hit rock bottom, losing a laugher to St. Louis 38–0. The loss dropped the Cowboys to 5–4 on the season, but it did wake them up. They won the rest of their regular season games to finish 10–4, and they advanced all the way to the Super Bowl before they were knocked off by the Baltimore Colts. The following year, Dallas went all the way, beating Miami 24–3 in Super Bowl VI.

### 3. 1973 MINNESOTA VIKINGS

The Vikings were well on their way to a fourth division title in five years and had a 10–1 record following a 9–0 start, as they entered a December contest with the Bengals in Cincinnati. It was there that Minnesota encountered a buzz saw. The Bengals, who had a pretty good team and ended up finishing 10–4, thumped the Vikings up and down the field at Riverfront Stadium, winning 27–0. The Vikings recovered to finish 12–2 and reach Super Bowl VIII, where they lost 24–7 to Miami.

### 4. 1973 MIAMI DOLPHINS

After a perfect 1972 season, the Dolphins lost a week two game the following season in Oakland by the count of 12–7. Miami then went on another streak, winning ten in a row to clinch the AFC East, the final two of those wins coming against quality opponents in Dallas and Pittsburgh. Most observers felt the Dolphins would breeze the rest of the way to the Super Bowl. But a week thirteen trip to Baltimore proved to be an eye opener. The lowly Colts, formerly coached by Miami head coach Don Shula, were on their way to a 4–10 season, but they held the Dolphins to just a Garo Yepremian field goal in a shocking 16–3 win. The loss must have jolted the Dolphins back to reality, as they cruised the rest of the way, culminating in a win over Minnesota in Super Bowl VIII.

## 5. 1976 OAKLAND RAIDERS

The Raiders started the 1976 season 3–0, but the games were all nailbiters that they won by a combined seven points. Come week four, though, their luck ran out as the Patriots, led by quarterback Steve Grogan, ambushed the Raiders 48–17 in Foxboro. That was the only loss of the season for Oakland, who finished 13–1, then trounced the Vikings in Super Bowl XI.

## 6. 1979 PITTSBURGH STEELERS

The three-time Super Bowl champion Steelers traveled to San Diego's Jack Murphy Stadium for a battle between two of the AFC's titans, and when they arrived, the Chargers served them a statement. With an offense led by Dan Fouts and a driven defense that forced eight Pittsburgh turnovers, including a spectacular 77-yard interception return for a touchdown by Woodrow Lowe, San Diego romped 35–7. The win helped earn San Diego home field advantage throughout the AFC playoffs. But before the teams could meet again in a playoff rematch, the Chargers were upset at home by the Oilers. Pittsburgh knocked off those same Oilers a week later on their way to a fourth Super Bowl championship.

## 7. 1992 BUFFALO BILLS

In an early season matchup at Rich Stadium, the rival Miami Dolphins laid a 37–10 whooping on the two-time defending AFC champion Bills. Safety Louis Oliver punctuated Miami's win with a 103-yard interception return for a touchdown. With the game well in hand, Oliver and a few of his defensive mates started dancing and singing on the sidelines in celebration. Yes, the Dolphins, who had not won a championship in a generation, were dancing. That act was not forgotten by the Bills, who later in the season beat the Dolphins in a prime time game in Miami. They dropped the Fish again in the AFC Championship Game, also played at Joe Robbie Stadium, by a score of 29–10. No dancing on the Bills sideline in either game.

## 8. 1990 NEW YORK GIANTS

Bill Parcells's Giants were riding high in the NFC East with a 10–0 record when they went into Philadelphia to face Buddy Ryan's Eagles. A potential matchup of unbeatens awaited them a week later in San Francisco, who also sported a perfect 10–0 record, but this game with a tough Philadelphia squad came first. Despite Parcells's success in New York, Ryan's Eagles always gave the Giants trouble and had beaten Big Blue four out of their previous five meetings. This day was no exception, as the offense, led by Randall Cunningham, put up four touchdowns, and the defense, spearheaded by Reggie White, harassed Phil Simms all afternoon long. The Giants' dreams of an unbeaten season ended with a humbling 31–13 loss and they finished up just 3–3 in their last six regular season games. But they regrouped in the postseason to beat the Bears and upset the 49ers and Bills to win their second Super Bowl in five years.

## 9. 1992 DALLAS COWBOYS

Jimmy Johnson's Cowboys were another team that struggled with the Eagles. His feud with Buddy Ryan was legendary, and at times he was pelted by debris, snow, and other objects by Philadelphia fans. By 1992, the Cowboys were on the verge of superstardom, but the Eagles, led by Rich Kotite (how's that for a shock, Jets fans) were a perennial playoff team, and they routed Dallas 31–7 in an early season game at Veterans Stadium. The Cowboys recovered to claim the Super Bowl championship.

## 10. 2003 NEW ENGLAND PATRIOTS

In week one of 2003 the Patriots were smoked by a Buffalo Bills team led by two determined ex-Patriots: quarterback Drew Bledsoe and safety Lawyer Milloy. Milloy was the more interesting of the two, having been cut by New England just days earlier in a salary dispute. He led a fierce defensive charge that hassled Tom Brady all day and kept the Patriots off the scoreboard. The highlight play of this game was Buffalo's 390- (or so) pound defensive tackle Sam Adams running back an interception for a touchdown, and somehow making it to the end zone without collapsing. The Bills won 31–0, but despite that hideous showing, the Pats recovered to win fourteen of their next fifteen games and knocked off Carolina to win the Super Bowl.

# Thieves

No play can change the fortunes of a game more quickly than a turnover. Here are ten of the NFL's most prolific pass interceptors.

### 1. PAUL KRAUSE
He picked off twelve passes as a Redskins rookie and kept on terrorizing quarterbacks for the remainder of his sixteen-year career, finishing as the all-time leader in interceptions with eighty-one. Krause missed only two games because of injury during his career, and that helped him bypass Emlen Tunnell for the all-time interception lead, as Krause broke the record with a two-pick game against the Rams late in 1979.

### 2. EMLEN TUNNELL
Emlen Tunnell, or Em, as teammates called him, changed the way people viewed safeties. During a fifteen-year career from 1948 through 1962 with both the Giants and Packers, Tunnell intercepted seventy-nine passes, two fewer than Krause, but Tunnell played two fewer seasons, and all but two of those were in twelve-game seasons. Tunnell did something remarkable in 1952 by gaining more yards on interception and kick returns than the league's rushing leader.

### 3. ROD WOODSON

Over a long career with the Steelers, 49ers, Ravens, and Raiders, Woodson had the knack for not only making the big interception, but also for getting a lot of yardage after the pick. Despite seventy-one career interceptions, Woodson never had a season with more than eight, a feat he accomplished twice. But he led the league twice and is the career record holder in touchdowns with twelve (three more than his nearest competition), and yards gained with 1,483 (201 more yards than Tunnell).

### 4. DICK "NIGHT TRAIN" LANE

Dick Lane was an undrafted veteran of the military when he tried out for the Los Angeles Rams in 1952. Good thing for the Rams they brought him in. His rookie season was a record breaker. Lane set an NFL record with fourteen interceptions in a 12-game season, a record remarkably still untouched for more than half a century, despite today's 16-game schedule. He played in seven Pro Bowls and finished with sixty-eight career interceptions and five touchdowns.

### 5. KEN RILEY

Riley was a standout cornerback for the Bengals for fifteen seasons from 1969 through 1983. In 1976 he set a Bengals single-season record with nine picks—which led the AFC—and was part of one of the best secondaries in the league, along with fellow cornerback Lamar Parrish and safety Tommy Casanova, who both made the Pro Bowl. He intercepted sixty-five passes in his career, returning five for touchdowns.

### 6. RONNIE LOTT

He was an intimidating force not only to opposing runners,

who felt his jarring hits, but also to opposing quarterbacks who tried to throw his way. Beginning with a Super Bowl championship rookie season with the 49ers in 1981 (when he intercepted 7 passes and returned three for touchdowns) until 1994 (when he played his final season with the New York Jets), Lott intercepted sixty-three passes, leading the league twice. He really made his mark in the postseason. In twenty playoff and Super Bowl contests, he intercepted nine passes and returned two for scores.

## 7. DAVE BROWN

How'd you like to go from one of the best football teams ever put together to an expansion franchise? That's what happened to Dave Brown, who played for the Steelers in 1975 in the team's Super Bowl X win over the Cowboys. The following off-season he was taken in the expansion draft by the Seattle Seahawks. That was a good move for Brown's career. He spent eleven years in the Pacific Northwest setting the Seahawks career mark with fifty interceptions. A career high-light was a two-touchdown game versus the Chiefs in 1984. He is one of six men in the Seahawks' Ring of Honor. Brown finished his career in 1990 with the Packers and is tied for seventh all-time with sixty-two interceptions.

## 8. DICK LeBEAU

Best known today as an innovative defensive coach, LeBeau was a standout cornerback for the Detroit Lions from 1959 through 1972, at one point playing in 171 consecutive games. That meant that the Lions had two of the most prolific thieves in history, LeBeau and Lane, in their starting secondary for six seasons. LeBeau finished his career with sixty-two picks and three touchdowns.

## 9. EMMITT THOMAS

Thomas, like Lane, was undrafted when he joined the Chiefs as a cornerback in 1966, but that did not stop him from having a prolific career. In his third season he led the AFL with nine interceptions, and in his fourth year, he had a fourth-quarter interception to seal the Chiefs' win over the Vikings in Super Bowl IV. His fifty-eight interceptions are ninth all-time and the most-ever by a Chief, surpassing by one the total of his secondary mate Johnny Robinson.

## 10. EVERSON WALLS

Walls is tied with Mel Blount, Bobby Boyd, Eugene Robinson, and the aforementioned Johnny Robinson for tenth all-time with fifty-seven interceptions. Walls is the only player to lead the league in picks three times, having done it in his rookie season of 1981, as well as in 1982 and 1985. He finished his career with the Giants and was a member of the Super Bowl XXV team that edged the Bills 20–19.

# When Number 1 Meets Number 2

Number 1 versus number 2. That's all you need to say when you're talking college football. There's no bigger game than when the top two teams in the polls meet on the field. It's made bigger by the fact that Division 1A football does not decide its champion via playoff, so the fan gets a real treat whenever number 1 plays number 2. In a later chapter we'll discuss the famous Thanksgiving Day 1971 contest between number 1 Nebraska and number 2 Oklahoma. Here are ten other classic number 1 versus number 2 matchups.

### 1. 1946—NUMBER 1 ARMY 0, NUMBER 2 NOTRE DAME 0

The country's best teams hooked up at Yankee Stadium in what was supposed to be a high octane offensive battle, since both teams averaged more than 30 points per game. Army was led by its star duo of "Mr. Inside," Doc Blanchard and "Mr. Outside," Heisman Trophy—winner Glenn Davis, while Notre Dame's big gun was quarterback Johnny Lujack. But the big story turned out to be the defenses, and the best player in the game was Army's Arnold Tucker, who had three interceptions. The scoreless tie stopped Army's 25-game winning streak and was more a "victory" for the Irish, who had been routed by the Cadets two years in a row. Notre Dame leap-frogged Army in the polls and won the national champion-ship, with Army right behind them at number 2.

## 2. 1969—NUMBER 1 TEXAS 15, NUMBER 2 ARKANSAS 14

Both teams had long winning streaks on the line for this December game in Fayetteville. Texas was riding high on an 18-game streak, while Arkansas had won fifteen in a row. The game was moved from its original date in October to December to accommodate all the attention it was sure to receive—which proved to be, as the game's television rating was an impressive fifty share. The Razorbacks had a 14–0 lead in the fourth quarter, but Texas quarterback James Street led the Longhorns back. First, he scored a 42-yard touch-down and added the 2-point conversion to make it a 14–8 game. Then Street completed a 44-yard pass on fourth and five to set up the winning touchdown by Jim Bertelson. The game gained even more notoriety by the presence of Presi-dent Nixon, who, following the game, anointed the Long-horns the national champion. Premature and unfair? Perhaps, since the bowls had yet to be played, and Penn State would also finish undefeated. But Texas finished its season with a win over Notre Dame in the Cotton Bowl and would have earned the title that way, anyhow.

## 3. 1966—NUMBER 1 NOTRE DAME 10, NUMBER 2 MICHIGAN STATE 10

This game goes down in history for what one of the teams did *not* do. With a sold out crowd at Spartan Stadium looking on, the score was tied in the fourth quarter. Notre Dame had possession of the ball at their own 30-yard line. With time left to mount a potential game-winning drive, Notre Dame head coach Ara Parsighian opted instead to run out the clock, preserving both the tie and his team's number one ranking. Critics and fans howled, but Parsighian countered that the Irish were without their top quarterback, Terry Hanratty, who was hurt when he was tackled by Bubba Smith earlier in the game, and they were also missing Nick Eddy, a starting running back who hurt his ankle stepping off the bus outside the stadium. The polls were status quo the rest of the season, with the Irish finishing on top and the Spartans maintaining their number 2 ranking.

## 4. 2003—NUMBER 2 OHIO STATE 31, NUMBER 1 MIAMI 24 (2 OT)

Miami took a 34-game winning streak into the BCS Championship Game at the Fiesta Bowl, but the unbeaten, underdog Buckeyes were not intimidated. After spotting the Hurricanes a 7–0 lead, Ohio State's stifling defense and opportunistic offense, led by quarterback Craig Krenzel and running back Maurice Clarett, took over the game. When a hideous knee injury knocked out Miami's star back Willis McGahee, the Canes looked to be in big trouble. But a big punt return by Roscoe Parrish late in the fourth quarter set up kicker Todd Sievers, who nailed a field goal to send the game into overtime. Miami quarterback Ken Dorsey then hit Kellen Winslow for a touchdown and a 24–17 lead. On OSU's first overtime possession, Krenzel kept the season alive with a fourth-and-fourteen completion to Michael Jenkins. Later in the drive, Krenzel again faced a fourth down, this time in a goal-to-go situation at the 5-yard line. His pass to the end zone went through the hands of Chris Gamble, who was heavily guarded by Glenn Sharpe. For a brief moment, Miami celebrated. But a late penalty flag flew in: defensive holding, first and goal Ohio State. Clarett punched it in from the 1-yard line to tie the game, and OSU went ahead on their possession in the second overtime. The Hurricanes advanced to a first and goal at the 1-yard line, but the Buckeyes held, and when Dorsey's final pass fell incomplete, Ohio State claimed a much-debated national championship.

## 5. 1988—NUMBER 1 NOTRE DAME 27, NUMBER 2 USC 10

In 1988 USC, Notre Dame, and UCLA all hovered near the top of the polls. Heading into November, the second-ranked Trojans had their destiny in their own hands: Beat number 1 Notre Dame at the Coliseum, knock off UCLA the following week, and beat the Big 10 champion in the Rose Bowl. It all seemed so simple until the Irish came to town. Backed by a potent defense and the spectacular play of quarterback Tony Rice, Notre Dame blindsided USC's national championship hopes with a 27–10 romp. A monster win over unbeaten West Virginia in the Fiesta Bowl a month later clinched another national championship for the Fighting Irish.

## 6. 1986—NUMBER 2 MIAMI 28, NUMBER 1 OKLAHOMA 16

In 1985 Barry Switzer's Oklahoma Sooners won the national championship with a record of 11–1. Their lone defeat came at the hands of Miami, 27–13, in an early season encounter in Norman. With revenge on their minds, the Sooners paid a visit to the Orange Bowl the following September in a game billed not only as number 1 versus number 2, but also as a battle of Heisman contenders: Miami quarterback Vinnie Testaverde and Oklahoma linebacker Brian Bosworth (don't chuckle, Bosworth was widely regarded as the most dominant defensive player in the nation). But as was the case the previous season, the Hurricanes proved to have too much speed on both sides of the ball and won rather convincingly. Interestingly, the teams would meet again in fifteen months on the same field, again number 1 versus number 2, this time in the Orange Bowl to decide the national championship. The Canes won that one, too, 20–14.

### 7. 1991—NUMBER 2 MIAMI 17, NUMBER 1 FLORIDA STATE 16

By 1991, Florida State had become one of the marquee college football programs, but there were two clouds that hung over Tallahassee: They couldn't win the national championship, and they couldn't beat Miami when it mattered. On a sunny afternoon perfect for football, the number 1 Seminoles, supported by a raucous home crowd, spotted Gino Torretta and the Hurricanes a 7–0 lead and then put the clamps on the Miami offense. Three field goals by Gerry Thomas and a touchdown run by Paul Moore gave FSU a 16–7 lead going into the fourth quarter. But Miami's clutch kicker Carlos Huerta nailed a big 45-yard field goal to cut the lead to six. On the next possession, Torretta led a heroic drive, culminating in a Larry Jones touchdown. The Hurricanes led by a point. Now trailing for the first time since the game's early stages, quarterback Casey Weldon led the Seminoles downfield inside the Miami 20-yard line with seconds on the clock. Thomas came on to attempt his fourth field goal, from 34 yards out. But he pushed it, just wide right, and the Hurricanes survived. They went on to share the national championship with Washington.

### 8. 1987—NUMBER 2 PENN STATE 14, NUMBER 1 MIAMI 10

The Miami Hurricanes entered the Fiesta Bowl carrying an enormous chip on their shoulders. Miami relished their "bad boy" image, right down to wearing fatigues to the Fiesta Bowl banquet. But this Miami team could back it up. They were loaded. They had the Heisman Trophy winner (Vinny Testaverde), three of the first ten picks in the upcoming draft (Testaverde, running back Alonzo Highsmith, and defensive lineman Jerome Brown), and a future Hall of Fame wide receiver (Michael Irvin). By contrast, their opponents, Penn State, were a little stale—more of a blue-blazer-and-khakis crowd. They didn't bring a lot of flash with them, but they did bring a defense that was the story of the game. Penn State picked off five Testaverde passes, including two by linebacker Pete Giftopolous, the second of which came near the goal line in the final seconds, preserving Joe Paterno's second national championship.

### 9. 1993—NUMBER 2 NOTRE DAME 31, NUMBER 1 FLORIDA STATE 24

Once again, the Seminoles came up on the short end of a game that was expected to have national championship ramifications. Florida State had gotten over one hurdle by beating Miami, and they were undefeated. But in a November game at Notre Dame Stadium the surprising Irish, also unbeaten, led throughout, echoing the glory of years past. They had to hold on, as Charlie Ward led a furious rally that came up short when his last-second pass to the end zone was knocked away. Notre Dame moved up to number 1, but they were knocked off the following week by Boston College. That enabled FSU to sneak back into the title picture, and their win over Nebraska in the Orange Bowl gave coach Bobby Bowden his first national championship—much to the chagrin of Irish fans.

### 10. 1989—NUMBER 1 NOTRE DAME 24, NUMBER 2 MICHIGAN 19

More than 105,000 braved the rain at The Big House to see the Wolverines welcome the top-ranked Irish. Raghib (the Rocket) Ismail of Notre Dame cemented his Heisman credentials by tying his own NCAA record with two kickoff returns for touchdowns as Notre Dame escaped with a 5-point win. Notre Dame would remain number 1 for much of the season until a late season loss to Miami.

# Memorable Movies

Hollywood and football do not always work well together (as you'll clearly see from the list that follows this one). But sometimes, everything comes together for a truly entertaining gridiron film. Here are some of Tinseltown's better football efforts.

## 1. *BLACK SUNDAY*

In a brilliant adaptation of Thomas Harris's chilling novel, Bruce Dern stars as a deranged blimp pilot who had been a POW during the Vietnam War. Still holding a grudge against the American government, he teams up with a Palestinian terror group in a plot to strap explosives to the blimp and detonate it at the Super Bowl. Robert Shaw plays an Israeli agent who is the only one who sees the enormity of the situation. Scenes from the film were shot at the Orange Bowl during Super Bowl X, but the scenes of panic in the crowd were shot separately.

## 2. *THE LONGEST YARD* (THE ORIGINAL)

Not just a funny football movie, this is hilarious whether you like the game or not. Burt Reynolds is Paul Crewe, a former NFL quarterback now behind bars. Eddie Albert, who everybody loved in *Green Acres*, plays the creepy Warden Hazen, whose pride and joy is his semipro football squad of guards. Warden Hazen sets up a game between the guards and a team of inmates, and he asks Paul to throw the game to win an early release. At first Paul has no use for the game, but soon he is torn between loyalty to his teammates and getting out. In the end, he sticks by his teammates in a great finish. The film had former NFL players Joe Kapp and Ray Nitschke among its cast.

### 3. *REMEMBER THE TITANS*

Based on a true story from 1971, *Remember the Titans* stars Denzel Washington as high school football coach Herman Boone. When two suburban Virginia schools (one predominantly black, one mostly white) are integrated, Boone is named coach over Bill Yoast, played by Will Patton, the head coach of the other school. Before the season begins, racism and fear run rampant, and some of the white players feel uneasy with a black coach. But beginning with summer practices, the team starts to grow together and they race through an undefeated season. When their star player is injured in an auto accident and can't play in the championship game, the team bands together to overcome their toughest challenge. Great performances by Washington and Patton make this an enjoyable movie for everybody.

### 4. *NORTH DALLAS FORTY*

Based on former Dallas Cowboy receiver Pete Gent's novel, *North Dallas Forty* is at times funny, at times raw, but it's one of the most realistic looks at life in the NFL. Nick Nolte and Mac Davis play for North Dallas, which is led by a cold, win-at-all-costs coach (who, not coincidentally, bears a striking resemblance to former Cowboys coach Tom Landry). Nolte is fabulous as an injured receiver who is shot up with all sorts of painkillers to keep him on the field. The film provides a scathing indictment of the lengths teams will go to win games. Former Raiders great-turned-actor John Matuszak had his most memorable role as a hot-headed lineman.

## 5. *JERRY MAGUIRE*

Although the phrase "chick flick" is often attached to this movie—which might scare off some football fans—this love story stars Tom Cruise as a player agent with only one client left, and Renee Zellweger as the one woman who stands by him during his worst times. It features a who's-who of the NFL: Dan Dierdorf, Frank Gifford, Wayne Fontes, Rick Mirer, Drew Bledsoe, Warren Moon, Dean Biasucci, Rich Kotite, Mel Kiper Jr., and Mel Kiper Jr.'s hair all make cameo appearances. Cuba Gooding Jr., won an Oscar in his role as Rod Tidwell, the only player still represented by Jerry Maguire. Jonathan Lipnicki steals all of his scenes as the young son of Zellweger's character (and since he's done very little else with his career, he will now forever carry the title of "that kid from *Jerry Maguire*").

## 6. *ALL THE RIGHT MOVES*

Made thirteen years prior to *Jerry Maguire*, this might be Tom Cruise's best football movie. Cruise is a senior football player in a Pennsylvania steel town, hoping for a scholarship to avoid the 9 to 5 union life that awaits those who don't go to college. Lea Thomson is his girlfriend, and Craig T. Nelson is perfect in his role as the high school coach who has a little too much power in his town. The clashes between Cruise and Nelson, as the player who wants to escape and the coach who can crush his ambitions, are the high points of the film.

## 7. *EVERYBODY'S ALL AMERICAN*

Dennis Quaid plays Gavin Grey, a superstar running back for LSU, who is greeted by adulation and fawning hero worship everywhere on campus. He dates the homecoming queen (Jessica Lange), and has the world at his feet. But when his pro career is halted by age and injury and the cheering stops, what happens next? Quaid and Lange are fabulous in the lead roles, and they are complemented by fine performances from Timothy Hutton as Gavin's cousin, and John Goodman, as Gavin's lineman, teammate, and best friend.

## 8. *BRIAN'S SONG*

If you're a guy, raise your hand if the first time you learned it was okay to cry was after watching this movie. A true story about the Bears' running back Brian Piccolo's battle with cancer, *Brian's Song* is a wonderful portrait of Piccolo's relationship with fellow running back Gale Sayers. With James Caan as Piccolo and Billy Dee Williams as Sayers, this movie about love, friendship, competition, and the will to fight to live, struck a chord with men everywhere.

## 9. *HEAVEN CAN WAIT*

The 1977–78 Rams are in the Super Bowl! Not for real, but in this delightfully breezy comedy based on the 1941 film *Here Comes Mr. Jordan*. Warren Beatty stars as the Rams quarterback who is taken out of his body before he's supposed to go. The star-studded cast includes Julie Christie, Jack Warden, and Charles Grodin.

## 10. *ANY GIVEN SUNDAY*

Though criticized in some circles for being bloated and boring, Oliver Stone's vibrant, violent film showed the raw side of life in the NFL. Al Pacino is the head coach of the Miami

Sharks, under pressure to win from his overbearing boss (Cameron Diaz) and forced to use his inexperienced backup quarterback (Jamie Foxx) when his veteran starter (Dennis Quaid) is hurt. Current and former NFL stars, among them Lawrence Taylor, Ricky Watters, Irving Fryar, Terrell Owens, and Jim Brown, added realism to the on-field scenes.

# Forgettable Football Flicks

Despite the list of films above, here's a general rule of thumb: If you're going to your local cineplex to see the latest movie and see that the subject matter is football, you might want to think twice about forking over your hard-earned money. That's because most football movies leave a lot to be desired. Here are some of Hollywood's football "bombs."

### 1. *THE BEST OF TIMES*
Robin Williams is Jack Dundee, a quiet banker with a shadow cast on his life: Back in high school, he bobbled a sure touchdown pass that cost his team the big game. Now saddled with the nickname "Butterfingers," Jack somehow convinces both sides to restage the game, bringing along his old buddy Reno, a quarterback played by Kurt Russell, on his quest for redemption. The movie climaxes with Jack making amends on a muddy field. *The Best of Times* is not the best effort from screenwriter Ron Shelton, who went on to direct the sports movies *Bull Durham* and *Tin Cup*.

## 2. *JOHNNY BE GOOD*

Johnny is the hottest high school quarterback prospect in the country, and with recruiting season starting to heat up, all the big colleges have come calling. With campus visits featuring booze- and girl-filled parties, will Johnny choose to go away to experience the wild life of college, or will he stay at a local school to be close to the girl of his dreams (played by a young Uma Thurman)? Seems like pretty standard Hollywood stuff, but Johnny is played by Anthony Michael Hall, who's about 115 pounds soaking wet, and who made a career out of playing a geek (*Sixteen Candles*, *The Breakfast Club*). Now all of a sudden we're supposed to believe he's the biggest jock in the country?

## 3. *LITTLE GIANTS*

Here's another peewee sport knock-off of *The Bad News Bears*. Danny O'Shea (Rick Moranis) has long been tormented by his older football star brother Kevin (Ed O'Neill). Now both are youth league coaches—Kevin with the best team in the league, and Danny with a team of lovable misfits. This all leads to the predictable "big game" scene, with the predictable finish.

## 4. *GUS*

The California Atoms stink. They can't win games and they can't draw any fans, and apparently all they need to do to improve is to get a better field goal kicker. So why not bring in a mule to kick and have his owner be the holder? When Gus, the mule, starts hitting 100-yard field goals, the team starts winning. How could a Disney flick with Don Knotts, Ed Asner, Tim Conway, Bob Crane, Richard Kiel, Dick Butkus, and John Unitas be bad? Easily.

### 5. *NECESSARY ROUGHNESS*

Hector Elizondo plays the head coach of the Texas State Fightin' Armadillos, and is he ever facing a long season. The NCAA has leveled heavy sanctions against the school and eliminated all scholarships, so the school must field a team from the student body. And with a matchup with top-ranked Texas coming up, they'll have to get by with a quarterback in his mid thirties (Scott Bakula), a female placekicker (Kathy Ireland, who's no Gus the Mule), and the rest of his motley crew, including Sinbad and Rob Schneider.

### 6. *THE REPLACEMENTS*

This is almost the professional football version of *Necessary Roughness*, only in this case the Washington Sentinels are facing a player strike. The team's owner (played by Gene Hackman) pulls together a ragtag bunch of replacement players led by Keanu Reeves as a former football hero searching for redemption. And of course the team starts to come together. Not much can really save this film—not even the numerous scenes of scantily-clad cheerleaders.

### 7. *THE PROGRAM*

James Caan plays the coach at a big-time college program that looks suspiciously like Florida State. Players and coaches face the pressures of school, then do things they shouldn't: playing highway "chicken," drinking, drugs, one even woos Halle Berry (actually, that's a good thing).

### 8. *NUMBER 1*

Charlton Heston plays Cat Catlan, a quarterback for the New Orleans Saints who's fallen into a depression. That's easy to do when you're playing for the Saints. His solution? Drinking and promiscuity. No wonder he's so washed up. Some of the scenes for this stinker were filmed on location in New Orleans's Tulane Stadium.

## 9. *WILDCATS*

Goldie Hawn plays Molly, a football fan and high school track coach who applies for the open football coach position at her school. Colleagues and players laugh when she applies, but when no real candidates emerge, the athletic director played by Nipsey Russell gives her the job. In the standard Hollywood story, the team (including early roles for Woody Harrelson and Wesley Snipes) resists her coaching, but once she proves herself, the team rallies around her.

## 10. *THE LONGEST YARD* (2005 REMAKE)

The summer of 2005 saw two great sports movies of the seventies remade with lackluster results: *The Bad News Bears* and *The Longest Yard*. Adam Sandler (he of *The Waterboy*) took on the Burt Reynolds role, and he just couldn't pull off the football scenes as Reynolds—who actually played football in college—did. And the rest of the cast, from Michael Irvin to Nelly to James Cromwell, just didn't stack up with the originals, despite having one of the funniest men alive—Chris Rock—along for the ride. So this can be added to the "unnecessary remakes of great films" Hall of Fame, along with *King Kong*, *Planet of the Apes*, *Psycho*, and *Godzilla*.

# Better Than Reading the Playbook

In the world of sports, it's generally accepted that the best books have been written about baseball. But that does not mean that there aren't books about football worth reading. Here are some of the better gridiron books to read on a rainy day.

## 1. *FRIDAY NIGHT LIGHTS*

In west Texas, high school football is king, and H. G. Bissinger brilliantly captures the hopes and dreams of the Panthers of Permian High. Bissinger chronicles one season through the eyes of a town and the mania that surrounds its team's every move. Packed houses of ten thousand or more are common. There are times when unemployment is so high that it seems the football team is the only thing the town has. The book is at its best as it examines the private lives of the players and the men and women who make Odessa, Texas run, as well as explores the social and racial divide of the town. But at its heart, it is a football story about how glory on the high school gridiron can be fleeting.

## 2. *PAPER LION*

The respected sportswriter Red Smith called George Plimpton's

*Paper Lion*, a first-person account of life in an NFL training camp, "the best book ever about pro football." Forty years after its first publication, few would argue. Plimpton was given the chance to take part in the Detroit Lions' summer camp as a 36-year-old rookie quarterback. Plimpton vividly chronicles everything he saw, from the rookie hazings to the constant drills to going face-to-face with All Pro Dick "Night Train" Lane. He stuck with the team right up through his pigskin highlight: an intra-squad scrimmage in Pontiac, Michigan, in which Plimpton didn't play all that well but learned a lot.

### 3. *INSTANT REPLAY*
Green Bay Packer guard Jerry Kramer's account of the 1967 season, cowritten with Dick Schaap, which culminated in a Super Bowl II win over the Oakland Raiders, is the seminal single-season football diary. Many have imitated—but none have surpassed—Kramer's account of training camp, life in Wisconsin, playing for Vince Lombardi, a devastating regular season loss to Johnny Unitas and the Colts in Baltimore, the Ice Bowl win over the Dallas Cowboys, and the camaraderie of the NFL locker room. Thirty years after this book was released, Kramer and Schaap revisited the Packers with the highly readable *Distant Replay*.

### 4. *JUNCTION BOYS*
In the sweltering summer of 1954, 100 football players went to Junction, Texas, to earn a spot on Paul "Bear" Bryant's Texas A&M squad, in Bryant's first season with the Aggies. After ten days of conditions that would have made a year's hard labor seem tame, only thirty-four remained. Jim Dent tells the compelling tale of those days, of the gritty players and the relentless coach. The 1954 team went only 1–9 that season, but it remained one of

TEXAS A&M MEDIA RELATIONS OFFICE

Paul "Bear" Bryant's early career at Texas A&M was turned into a best-selling book and ESPN movie, The Junction Boys.

Bryant's favorite teams to coach, and they formed the nucleus of a team that would go undefeated two seasons later.

### 5. *WHEN PRIDE STILL MATTERED*
In perhaps the best-written football biography ever, Pulitzer Prize-winning author David Maraniss captures the essence of the man who helped transform the NFL in the 1960s: Vince Lombardi. From Lombardi's hardscrabble roots in New York, through his college years at Fordham, to his time in Green Bay where he won five championships in nine years, Maraniss brilliantly evokes the man who was respected by all.

### 6. *YOU'RE OK, IT'S JUST A BRUISE*
Rob Huizenga was a young doctor who thought he'd landed a dream job in 1983: team internist for the Los Angeles Raiders. But he discovered a culture of steroid and drug abuse among players, coaches who wanted their players on the field at all costs, and team doctors and owners turning a blind eye to their players' health. And when he voiced his concerns, he found a nemesis: Raiders' owner Al Davis, who liked his doctors to treat the players quickly and get them back between the lines.

### 7. *NAMATH: A BIOGRAPHY*
It's booze, broads, and Broadway, baby! New York sports-writer Mark Kriegel brings the legend—and the truth—of "Broadway" Joe Namath vividly to life. From a childhood of hustling in a broken home in Beaver Falls, Pennsylvania, through college under Bear Bryant at Alabama, and the bright lights of New York, Kriegel tells the story of an immensely talented player struggling with injuries who just wanted to have a good time. Here is Namath at his flamboyant best, guaranteeing a win for the Jets in Super Bowl III, but here also is

Namath at his career low, stuck as a backup to Pat Haden with the Rams.

### 8. *THE DARK SIDE OF THE nFL*

Tim Green played eight NFL seasons before retiring to become an attorney and a television analyst. He also went on to write a number of popular novels, but his most famous book was his exposé on life as a player in the NFL. Green describes the day-to-day existence of a football player as it really is— and that fans don't see on television. Steroids and other performance enhancing drugs, gambling, racism, alcohol, injuries, even why training camp is a big waste of time—Green covers them all to give fans an inside look at the NFL's dark side.

### 9. *nEVER DIE EASY*

Walter Payton may have been the best all-around offensive player of the last fifty years. Consider: He retired as the league's all-time leading rusher, he was one of the best blocking backs of his time, and he was the Bears' all-time leading receiver, to boot. But the man they called "Sweetness" was a warm man who valued his family life much more than any records he achieved on the field. His autobiography, written with Don Yaeger, reveals the man—on and off the field—whose most heroic battle was with the illness that finally took his life.

### 10. *I AM THIRD*

Gale Sayers of the Chicago Bears wrote this inspirational memoir about his life and career. Despite his career being cut short due to knee injuries, and one of his best friends, teammate Brian Piccolo, succumbing to cancer, Sayers never lost sight of his faith. The title of the book came from a saying of Sayers's: "The Lord is first, my friends are second, and I am third."

# Super Significant Others

L et's face it, being a star professional football player has its advantages. The money is great, and really beautiful women start to pay attention to you. Here are ten football pros who wound up with some of the entertainment world's most alluring women.

## 1. BOB WATERFIELD

He was a professional football Hall of Famer and spouse of one of the most recognized bombshells of the 1940s and 1950s. Not a bad life if you can lead it, and Bob Waterfield did. He quarterbacked the Los Angeles Rams, twice going to the Pro Bowl and once winning the league MVP in 1945. But in what may be an even more impressive feat, he wed Hollywood starlet Jane Russell in 1943. Russell, remembered for roles in films such as *Gentlemen Prefer Blondes*, and Waterfield were married for twenty-five years.

## 2. FRANK GIFFORD

He played college ball in Los Angeles at the University of Southern California and had a Hall of Fame career in New York with the Giants, but living as a star in those media centers did not give Frank Gifford a fraction of the spotlight he would get in his marriage. In 1986 Gifford was one of the announcers on Monday Night Football, and Kathie Lee Johnson was a singer and television personality just a few years shy of her really big break, when the two wed. By 1990, Kathie Lee was the cohost of a popular morning television show with Regis Philbin, where she talked about Frank and their kids all the time (practically every day). By the late 1990s, allegations of an affair by Frank and the purported use of sweatshops by makers of Kathie Lee's clothing line put strains on their marriage and put them in the tabloids on a daily basis. But the marriage lasted, and the two are still together as of this writing.

### 3. **AHMAD RASHAD**

After finishing off an eleven-year career with the Cardinals, Bills, and Vikings, Ahmad Rashad embarked on a sports casting career. One of his first jobs was at NBC, as part of their NFL studio show hosted by Bob Costas. By 1985, he was dating one of the most popular women on the network, Phylicia Ayers-Allen, who was playing Mrs. Huxtable on *The Cosby Show*. They became engaged on national television on Thanksgiving Day 1985 when Ahmad, as part of NBC's coverage of the Jets–Lions game, proposed on the air. Though the acceptance wasn't televised, Phylicia said yes, and the couple were married sixteen years before divorcing.

### 4. **JOE THEISMANN**

In the early 1980s, Joe Theismann was riding high. His Redskins were perennial contenders, winning Super Bowl XVII and losing the next year to the Raiders in Super Bowl XVIII. His personal life was looking pretty good, too. For seven years, Theismann squired actress Cathy Lee Crosby around.

Crosby was remembered best as one of the cohosts of ABC's variety program *That's Incredible*. Interestingly, one of her cohosts was another Super Bowl quarterback, Fran Tarkenton. Crosby's career breakout was in 1974's television movie version of *Wonder Woman*.

### 5. ANDRE RISON

In the early 1990s, wide receiver Andre Rison put up big numbers in the run and shoot offense of the Atlanta Falcons. At around that time, Rison began a relationship with Lisa "Left Eye" Lopes, one of the members of the enormously popular musical trio known as TLC. TLC hit its peak with 1994's number 1 hit *Waterfalls*, from the album *CrazySexyCool*. Left Eye was certainly sexy and cool. She proved herself to be crazy, too, when she set fire to the Atlanta mansion she shared with Rison. The house burned to the ground, but the relationship didn't burn with it. Rison stuck with Lopes on and off over the following years. A planned 2001 wedding was cancelled, and any hopes of reconciliation ended when Lopes was tragically killed in a car accident in Honduras in 2002.

### 6. RODNEY PEETE

After starring for some pretty good USC teams in the 1980s, quarterback Rodney Peete had a relatively long journeyman career in the NFL, with stops in Detroit, Dallas, and Carolina, to name a few. He completed a lot of passes over the years, but his best hook up came in 1993 when he met the beautiful actress Holly Robinson, famous for her roles on the television programs *21 Jump Street* and *Hangin' with Mr. Cooper*. The couple wed in 1995 and remain together.

### 7. JASON SEHORN

Though he was a cornerback for the New York Giants, Jason

Sehorn's wife grew up a Cowboys fan. That would be Angie Harmon, whose acting career got a jumpstart on the forgettable *Baywatch Nights* before starring on *Law & Order*. Harmon accepted Sehorn's marriage proposal live on *The Tonight Show* before a surprised Jay Leno and national television audience. While in the midst of an interview, Harmon was interrupted by Sehorn getting down on one knee. And she said yes.

### 8. TIM HASSELBECK
Hasselbeck married his college sweetheart, Elisabeth Filarski, after her appearance on *Survivor: The Australian Outback,* where she finished fourth. A quarterback for the Redskins, Hasselbeck was in his first season in D.C. when Elisabeth won a slot on *The View*.

### 9. TIM COUCH
Life's not easy for the number one overall pick in the draft. At least that's true in the case of Tim Couch, the first player taken in 1999. Couch had an up-and-down five seasons with the Cleveland Browns. Along the way, he lost his starting job and almost lost his girlfriend. Couch was seeing Heather Kozar, a beautiful blonde who was a former Playmate and *Price is Right* model. Couch made the mistake of introducing Kozar to Cade McCown, a friend and fellow quarterback draftee, who promptly made a move on her. McCown, who turned out to be a bigger stiff in the NFL than Couch, and Kozar were together briefly before she returned to Couch. And he took her back! I guess there are advantages to being a Playmate, too. Kozar and Couch were married in 2005.

### 10. MARK GASTINEAU
After a messy divorce from his wife Lisa in the 1980s, Jets

defensive end Mark Gastineau hooked up with actress Brigitte Nielsen, the former wife of Sylvester Stallone. Gastineau and Nielsen were together for three years, from 1988 through 1990, but never married.

# Would You Buy What This Man Is Selling?

Companies love to use a famous athlete as their spokes-person in television commercials. Following is a list of some of the more memorable, or maybe forgettable, spots featuring football players.

### 1. MEAN JOE GREENE

The scene is a dark tunnel under a loud grandstand. The Pittsburgh Steelers' Mean Joe Greene limps toward the locker room, when suddenly a little boy appears and offers him his Coca-Cola. That simple premise became one of the most famous commercials in television history. In fact, *TV Guide* ranked it as one of its fifty best commercials of all time. America warmed watching the icy Greene's heart melt as he chugged the kid's bottle of Coke. Then, as the spot concludes, Mean Joe says, "Hey, kid, catch!" and tosses his jersey to the boy.

### 2. JOE NAMATH

Boy, did Joe Namath selling pantyhose ever cause a stir! The Jets quarterback made a commercial for Beautymist pantyhose in 1974, in which he actually wore the product. The spot opens with a shot of a pair of legs and slowly reveals green shorts and a New York Jets number 12 jersey, before we see that it's actually Namath. The message is that if these can make Joe Willie's legs look good, then imagine what they can do for you! It was a bold move by Namath and it paid off, as many people still remember him more for this commercial than anything he ever did on a football field.

### 3. BO JACKSON

For a few years back in the late 1980s and early 1990s, it seemed that Bo knew just about everything. Two-sport star Bo Jackson was a commercial spokesperson for Nike and was the star of the famous "Bo knows" series of ads. We all knew that Bo knew baseball and football, but thanks to these commercials, we found out that Bo knows tennis, Bo knows golf, Bo knows cycling (look out, Lance Armstrong!)—Bo even knows polo. Bo knew business and how to market himself, that's for sure. One humorous spot concluded with Bo holding an electric guitar and butchering whatever he was trying to play. Then we see a real guitar legend, Bo Diddley, sitting next to him, who yells "Bo, you don't know diddley!"

### 4. DAN MARINO

Every year around the holiday season, Dan Marino appeared on television selling Isotoner gloves. Dan told the audience that he always gave his receivers and linemen Isotoner gloves as gifts because it was important to take care of the hands that took care of him. Marino also appeared in an Isotoner "commercial" in the movie *Ace Ventura, Pet Detective*.

### 5. THE OLD MILLER LITE ADS

"Tastes great! Less filling! Tastes great! Less filling!" That was the argument in the classic Miller Lite ads when posed with the question of what makes Miller Lite better than all the other beers. The Miller Lite ads were a series of commercials with a large roster of athletes and former athletes from the major sports, including a number from the NFL, among them Dick Butkus. Another football player in the spots was Bubba Smith, whose classic line was that he "loved the easy opening cans," as he ripped said can in half. Don't forget the former Raider Ben Davidson, who reminded Rodney Dangerfield at a bowling match that "all we need is one pin, Rodney!" just before poor Rodney pings the ball off the head pin without knocking any down. But the Miller Lite commercials were a launching pad for the career of John Madden. Madden was always at his frenetic best, and his spots often culminated in him crashing through the backdrop yelling, "Hey, wait a minute!" as the commercial went off the air.

## 6. GARO YEPREMIAN

Whoever said that being a bonehead couldn't pay off? Garo Yepremian, the former placekicker for the Dolphins, is best remembered for his blunder in Super Bowl VII that cost his team seven points. With the Dolphins ahead of the Redskins 14–0 in the fourth quarter, Yepremian had a game-clinching field goal blocked, retrieved the loose ball, attempted a forward pass (to whom, it's never quite been revealed), only to have that slip out of his hands and batted into the arms of Washington's Mike Bass, who scampered 49 yards for a touchdown to give the Redskins brief hope. Garo's folly made him a national celebrity, much to the chagrin of Dolphins teammates, who still to this day haven't forgiven him for what he did (and these are the guys who *won* the game!). Garo capitalized on this sudden fame with an appearance on *The Odd Couple* and in a commercial for Right Guard with Oakland tight end Dave Casper back in the 1970s. Garo extols the virtues of Right Guard's new product, the Power Pump antiperspirant spray, showing how much more effective it is than Casper's Ban Basic.

### 7. WILLIAM "THE REFRIGERATOR" PERRY

Back in 1985, Fridge Perry made a splash on the national scene as a rookie defensive tackle with the Super Bowl champion Bears. His size and celebrity made him a perfect spokesman for McDonald's, who used the Fridge to help launch their new "McDLT" sandwich. The McDLT had unique packaging, as the toppings and the top of the bun rested in a separate compartment from the patty and the bun, so "the hot stays hot, and the cool stays cool." In his spot, Fridge goes to the local McDonald's with friends for a little lunch, and the counter girl repeats his order for all of us to hear: "That's 4 McDLTs, two large fries, and a *diet* Coke?" Then Fridge goes to take his seat and can barely fit into his booth. Boy, fat guys are just hilarious, aren't they? Despite the funny commercial with the Fridge, the McDLT never quite caught on and was removed from the McDonald's menu. Interestingly, McDonald's ran other ads for the McDLT featuring a then-unknown actor: a pre-George Costanza Jason Alexander.

### 8. TOM LANDRY

He was a quiet, stoic man who may have been the best coach in NFL history. So it was surprising to see the Cowboys' coach appearing in one of those "Do you know me?" commercials for American Express, especially dressed in a cowboy get-up. Landry explains why it's so important to have the security of the American Express card at your disposal, because "you never know when you'll be surrounded by Redskins," as a group of guys in Redskins uniforms form a circle around him.

## 9. TERRY BRADSHAW

The folks at 1-800-Collect decided they needed to find celebrities from the fields of sports and entertainment to sell their product, so they went with these three icons: Terry Bradshaw, Hall of Fame quarterback and professional buffoon; "Alf," a puppet from outer space (well, check that, he's just a puppet, but the character Alf was from outer space on a show that was on TV back in the early 1980s); and All Star catcher Mike Piazza, who sported a "When am I getting the check for this?" look on his face. The ads ran for a few years, and 1-800-Collect also recruited Emmitt Smith of the Cowboys for a couple of spots.

## 10. MICHAEL VICK

Can Falcons quarterback Michael Vick knock his receivers on their backs with a pass, or throw a bomb completely out of the stadium? As unlikely (read: impossible) as this is, in a commercial for Powerade, Vick does just that. Thanks to some clever use of digital editing, the passes all look real. It was so clever, in fact, that many believed the footage to be authentic. This was an effective campaign for Powerade, one that they used again in a followup spot with Lebron James, in which Lebron hits a series of jump shots from the other end of the court.

# Going Long

If you include the two end zones, a football field is 120 yards long, but it's pretty rare to see a play longer than 25 to 30 yards. There are times when a player makes a long gain and puts a dagger into the opposition. Here are ten plays that covered big chunks of yardage.

### 1. CHRIS MCALISTER

On a Monday night in week three of the 2002 season, Baltimore defensive back Chris McAlister scooped up an errant field goal attempt by Denver's Jason Elam and raced into the record books. With time running out in the first half, the Broncos, trailing 24–3, lined up for a 57-yard field goal attempt by Elam. When the kick came up short, McAlister waited momentarily, picked up the ball, got behind a wall of purple jerseys, followed a crushing block by Ray Lewis, and scampered untouched 108 yards for a touchdown—the longest score of any kind in NFL history. McAlister's feat was matched in 2005 by the Chicago Bears' Nathan Vasher, who returned a missed field goal 108 yards against the 49ers.

### 2. TONY DORSETT

You couldn't get more pinned back in your own side of the

field than the Cowboys. Backed up about a foot from their own goal line, they looked to be in big trouble against the Minnesota Vikings. It was the final regular season game of 1982 on a Monday night in the Metrodome. Dorsett took a handoff from a couple of yards in the end zone, exploded through a hole on the right side of the offensive line and was off to the races. He shook off one last pursuer near the Minnesota 25-yard line and stayed on his feet for a 99-yard run, the longest run from scrimmage in NFL history.

### 3. ERIC CROUCH

It's sometimes said that winners of the Heisman Trophy have a signature play during their magical season. In 1984 Doug Flutie had the Hail Mary in Miami, and in 2001 Eric Crouch had The Run at Missouri, part of a 36–3 Cornhuskers win. With Nebraska back on their own 5-yard line in the third quarter, Crouch dropped back to pass. He scrambled back near the goal line, looking for a receiver, and barely escaped a sack. When no one got open, Crouch, who possessed the speed of a tailback, took off up the middle. He avoided the pursuing Missouri secondary and ran all the way to the end zone for a Nebraska-record 95-yard run.

### 4. STEVE O'NEAL

In just the second game of his NFL career, Steve O'Neal set a record that will be very difficult to break. During a September 21, 1969 game against the Broncos at Mile High Stadium, O'Neal, the punter for the Jets, found himself kicking from his own end zone as the Jets had a fourth down on their 1-yard line. O'Neal boomed the ball past midfield and, upon landing, it took a fortuitous Jets bounce. The ball rolled and rolled, finally coming to rest at the Denver 1, for a record-setting 98-yard punt.

### 5. **GARRISON HEARST**

Opening Day 1998 was an offensive shootout between the San Francisco 49ers and the New York Jets. Steve Young and Glenn Foley had big games passing for each team, and the game went to overtime tied at 31. Both teams exchanged possessions, before the 49ers took over at their own 4-yard line following a Jets punt. On the next play, San Francisco's Garrison Hearst took a handoff and went off tackle to the right. After avoiding a tackle at the line of scrimmage, Hearst shed Jets free safety Kevin Williams near the 20 and was off to the races. Hearst outran linebacker Mo Lewis, who finally tracked Hearst down near the goal line, but it was too late, as Hearst's momentum carried the tackler with him into the end zone for a game-winning 96-yard touchdown.

### 6. **TONY MARTIN**

In 1994, just two weeks after Chargers defensive back Stanley Richard returned an interception 99 yards for a touchdown against the Broncos, the San Diego offense matched that same yardage output. Playing the Seahawks at Husky Stadium and wearing their throwback white helmets, quarterback Stan Humphries connected with wide receiver Tony Martin on a 99-yard touchdown pass to help lead the Chargers to a 27–10 win.

### 7. **CLIFF BRANCH**

The Washington Redskins and Los Angeles Raiders faced off in one of the best regular season games of the 1983 season. In a game of big plays and momentum swings, the longest play came courtesy of two grizzled veterans of the Raiders. Wide receiver Cliff Branch caught a bomb from Jim Plunkett and raced into the end zone at RFK stadium with a 99-yard touchdown. More remarkable about the play was that Branch hurt his hamstring but still reached paydirt.

### 8. MIKE QUICK

In a 1985 clash with the Falcons, the Eagles found themselves backed up at their own 1-yard line in overtime. Philadelphia had to be concerned, for in this spot a botched snap or an end zone penalty would result in a sudden loss. But just when it looked hopeless, Philly quarterback Ron Jaworski dropped back to pass and hit wide receiver Mike Quick in stride over the middle. Quick avoided a would-be tackler and raced the length of the field for the decisive 99-yard touchdown, the longest play from scrimmage in NFL overtime history.

### 9. ROBERT BROOKS

A talented Packers team was locked in a tight duel with the Bears on a 1995 Monday Night at Soldier Field. Green Bay was able to escape with a 27–24 win, due in no small part to a little Brett Favre magic. From his own 1-yard line, Favre dropped back and saw Robert Brooks isolated on the right sideline. Favre dropped a spiral right in Brooks's arms, and he raced untouched the rest of the way for a 99-yard touchdown.

### 10. ED REED

In a 2004 game at PSINet Stadium in Baltimore, the Cleveland Browns trailed the Ravens by a touchdown late in the fourth quarter, but they were driving deep into Ravens territory. With the ball at the 5-yard line, quarterback Jeff Garcia threw toward Aaron Shea in the middle of the end zone. But the ball arrived at the same time as linebacker Ray Lewis, whose hit caused Shea to tip the ball in the air. Safety Ed Reed snatched the deflection out of the air and raced 106 yards down the sideline to clinch a 27–13 win. It was the longest interception return in NFL history by three yards, surpassing returns by Miami's Louis Oliver and San Diego's Vencie Glenn.

# Before the Legends

We all know who the legendary coaches are, but they had to get a start at some point, and that came when another coach had to be removed. The following ten men were all replaced by some of the greatest coaches in football history.

### 1. GEORGE WILSON

When Joe Robbie brought an expansion franchise to the AFL and South Florida in 1966, he turned to a former NFL coach with a championship to his credit. In eight seasons coaching the Detroit Lions, George Wilson won fifty-five games, lost forty-five, and tied six, and he led them to the NFL championship in 1957—the last time any Lions team won a title.

On his staff in Motown was a young defensive assistant named Don Shula. As the head man for Robbie's expansion Miami Dolphins, Wilson struggled, going 15–39–2 in four years, before he was fired. Robbie found Wilson's replacement in Baltimore head coach Don Shula, the same man who had been an assistant under Wilson in Detroit. The rest is history.

## 2. **FRED O'CONNOR**

The San Francisco 49ers hit rock bottom in the 1970s. Following an 8–5–1 record in 1972, they suffered through six years of misery, culminating in a disastrous 2–14 in 1978. During that season, Pete McCulley was let go after a 1–8 start, and Fred O'Connor finished out the year. O'Connor's replacement also had a rough go of it in his first year at the helm, likewise finishing 2–14 in 1979, but he had a little more luck with things after that. His name? Bill Walsh.

## 3. **RAY "SCOOTER" MCLEAN**

A former assistant with the Green Bay Packers, McLean became the Packers' head coach in 1957. Good thing for Packer faithful that McLean had a dreadful 1–10–1 season. That gave the team the opportunity to get rid of him after one year and hire the best available candidate: New York Giants assistant Vince Lombardi. This hire was significantly better, to say the least, as Lombardi would go on to win five titles in Green Bay.

## 4. **RICH KOTITE**

Following a 6–10 season in 1994, Leon Hess, the aging owner of the New York Jets, fired Pete Carroll as head coach after only one year. Hess hired the recently released coach of the Eagles, Rich Kotite, a former assistant in New York who lost his final seven games in Philadelphia. Hess's reasoning? He said, "I'm eighty years old; I want results now!" Well, in two years under Kotite, the Jets' results were pretty dismal: his record was 4–28. Add that to his final seven games with the Eagles, and you get 4–35. Kotite left the team following the 1996 season saying, "I didn't quit, and I wasn't fired," (whatever that means). Hess then turned to a man who really could produce results: Bill Parcells, who coached the Jets to their first division championship in twenty-nine years in 1998.

## 5. BILL AUSTIN

The late 1960s were business as usual for the Pittsburgh Steelers. In other words, they lost—a lot. Under Bill Austin they went 11–28–3 in three seasons from 1966–1968. His run ended with a 2–11–1 campaign in 1968. That led owner Art Rooney to make a change to Baltimore assistant Chuck Noll, a man who had served in a winning program under Don Shula. Good move! Noll would win four Super Bowl championships in the next twelve seasons.

## 6. GERRY FAUST

Before Lou Holtz returned the Notre Dame Fighting Irish to the national championship stage in the late 1980s, the Irish had one of their worst stretches in the years 1981–1985. That's when Gerry Faust, the former head coach at Cincinnati prep powerhouse Moeller High, was the Notre Dame head man. Faust went 30–26–1 during his tenure, including a humiliating 58–7 loss in his final game at Miami—and that just doesn't cut it at the Golden Dome.

## 7. HANK BULLOUCH

Bullouch had a couple of rough years in Buffalo, and not only because of the weather. He went 2–10 over the final twelve games of 1985, and 2–7 in the first nine games of 1986, before he was fired. The Bills turned to former Chiefs coach Marv Levy, who guided the Bills to eight playoff appearances and four straight Super Bowl appearances.

## 8. RIP ENGLE

If you know that Rip Engle is the man whom Joe Paterno

replaced as head coach of Penn State football in 1966, you either know an awful lot about football or you're a PSU alum. In 1944 Engle was named head coach at Brown, where he stayed for six years; one of his players was a young Joe Paterno. In 1950 Engle moved to Penn State where he hired the 23-year-old Paterno as an assistant. In sixteen years in Happy Valley, Engle had a record of 104–48–4. After his retirement, Paterno took over and he's been at Penn State ever since.

## 9. DARRELL MUDRA

In 1973 Darrell Mudra began his fourth collegiate head coaching job. He first led North Dakota State and Arizona before a successful five-year stint at Western Illinois, where his worst season was 7–3. But Mudra had no such success at his fourth school, Florida State University. In two seasons he won just four games and was replaced by West Virginia coach Bobby Bowden, who's now been in Tallahassee for more than thirty years and two national championships. Mudra got back into coaching, leading Eastern Illinois and Northern Iowa for five seasons each. In twenty-two total seasons as a head coach, Mudra won 168 games and had seven years in which his team won ten or more games.

## 10. JACK PARDEE

Pardee had been a star linebacker for the Redskins and was the anchor of their defense in Super Bowl VII. He was named their head coach before the start of the 1978 season. Following three unspectacular, yet not dreadful, seasons in which he went 24–24 (and helped along the development of quarterback Joe Theismann), he was fired. The move was controversial to many, and the complaints only grew louder when the new coach started his first year 0–5. His name? Joe Gibbs.

# After the Legends

$C$oaches don't last forever . . . even the really good ones. And when they do go, someone is faced with the unenviable task of replacing a legend. Here are ten coaches who did just that, and how they fared.

## 1. PHIL BENGSTON

How do you replace Vince Lombardi? That's got to be like taking the stage after the Beatles, as Bengston found out in 1968. He lasted three years as head coach of the Packers, and his record wasn't terrible, but 20–21–1 wasn't going to make anyone forget Lombardi. A 40–0 home opening loss to the Lions in 1970 may have been one of the final straws that led to his firing.

## 2. RAY PERKINS

Following the retirement of Bear Bryant after the 1982 season, one of his former players (and New York Giants head coach), Ray Perkins, became the head man at the University of Alabama. Perkins had a solid four seasons, going 32–15–1 with three bowl wins in three chances, but no SEC championships. He was replaced for the 1987 season by Bill Curry.

### 3. CHARLIE WINNER

When Hall of Famer Weeb Ewbank stepped aside as head coach of the New York Jets after the 1973 season, he stayed on as GM—meaning he would be hiring his replacement. Now, Weeb could have tapped one of his long-time assistants, Chuck Knox or Walt Michaels. But these were the Jets, after all. So Weeb hired Charlie Winner. Who? Well, Charlie had been a head coach before with St. Louis for five seasons, where his record was okay (35–30–3). But he also had another vital quality: He was Weeb's son-in-law. Let's just say that Winner didn't exactly live up to his name, going 9–14 before being dismissed.

### 4. LES STECKEL

Following the 1983 season, Bud Grant finally called it quits from the Vikings, after guiding Minnesota to four Super Bowl appearances. The Vikings called on a young disciplinarian, Les Steckel, as their new head coach, but his iron fist quickly wore thin with players. Minnesota dropped to 3–13 in Steckel's only season. The situation was such a mess that Grant himself came out of retirement to take over for the 1985 season.

### 5. RAY HANDLEY

There was speculation after Bill Parcells won his second Super Bowl with the Giants in 1990 that he might retire, but he didn't make a final decision until a few months later. By that time, star defensive coordinator Bill Belichick had taken the Cleveland Browns job, so GM George Young turned to running back coach Ray Handley. That proved to be a huge mistake, as Handley was ill-equipped to handle the New York media and a budding quarterback controversy between Phil Simms and Jeff Hostetler. Handley was fired after two years and a 14–18 record.

### 6. GENE RONZANI

At the end of the 1949 season there were two men considered the legendary coaches of the NFL. One was George Halas, who had coached on and off since the early 1920s, and the other was Green Bay's Earl "Curly" Lambeau. The task of taking Lambeau's place fell to Ronzani. In his four years in Green Bay the Pack struggled, going 14–33–1 before he was let go.

### 7. EARL BRUCE

Woody Hayes was removed from his position as head coach at Ohio State after an incident in the 1978 Gator Bowl, in which he came off the sideline to punch a Clemson player. The legendary Hayes was replaced by his former assistant, Earl Bruce. In nine years under Bruce, the Buckeyes played in eight bowl games and either won or shared the Big Ten title four times. Bruce's record in Columbus was a robust 81–26–1.

### 8. JIM DOOLEY

So who could replace the Bears' George Halas when he retired for good with the most all-time wins? That fell to Jim Dooley. Dooley's first year was fair, going 7–7, but in 1969 he went 1–13 (with Dick Butkus and Gale Sayers!). With the Vikings emerging as the power team in the division, Dooley's Bears fell to consecutive 6–8 seasons in 1970 and 1971, and he was fired.

### 9. BILL JOHNSON

When Paul Brown retired from the Cincinnati Bengals after an 11–3 season in 1975, the Bengals could have hired one of Brown's offensive disciples, a guy by the name of Bill Walsh. But, alas, they chose Johnson instead. The team did quite well in his first two years, going 10–4 and 8–6, but missing the playoffs (remember these were the glory years of the Steelers). When the Bengals stumbled out of the gate 0–5 in 1978, Johnson was canned.

## 10. DON MCCAFFERTY

How many coaches can replace an icon (Don Shula), go 21–6–1 over their first two seasons with a Super Bowl championship one year, and a trip to the conference championship game in the next, only to be fired the subsequent season? That's what happened to McCafferty, who, two years after winning Super Bowl V with the Colts was fired after a 1–4 start. That was the first season under new ownership in Baltimore, after owner Carroll Rosenbloom swapped franchises with the Rams' Bob Irsay, so the new ownership was looking for any excuse to get its own guy in there. And no, the Colts have never won another Super Bowl.

# Strange Team Nicknames

In my earlier book, *Super Bowl's Most Wanted*, I listed some players with bizarre names and nicknames who took the field on Super Bowl Sunday. This list includes some of the more peculiar team names and nicknames, from the college and pro ranks.

## 1. OORANG INDIANS

An NFL team in 1922 and 1923, they boasted Jim Thorpe and a roster of Native American players (hence the nickname Indians). The team was basically a front to publicize the owner's prized kennel, the Oorang Dog Kennels in LaRue, Ohio. The team only won four games in two seasons, before folding up shop. But here's a question: Why not name the team the Oorang Utans? Didn't anybody in the front office have a sense of humor?

## 2. PROVIDENCE STEAM ROLLER

Those teams back in the 1920s sure had a flair for wild names, huh? The Steam Roller played from 1925 through 1931 and even won a title in 1928. Playing their games in a stadium built for bicycle races, they were the first team to play an NFL game under the lights. It was a 1929 contest against the Chicago Cardinals that the Steam Roller lost 16–0, but it drew 6,000 fans—a large number at the time.

### 3. DELAWARE BLUE HENS

Think of some of the powerful nicknames in football. Raiders, Lions, Giants, Bears—Blue Hens? Though it's not very menacing, the nickname didn't hurt the University of Delaware in 2003 when they won the Division IAA national championship. But where did the nickname Blue Hens come from? Back during the Revolutionary War, the Continental Army's Delaware units had an interesting way to amuse themselves: by staging cockfights featuring Blue Hens. Don't get any ideas —cockfighting (and Blue Hen fighting) is now illegal in most places.

### 4. TCU HORNED FROGS

Frogs don't really have horns, do they? Well, at Texas Christian University they do. It's not likely that a frog would intimidate anyone, even with horns. The horned frog in nature is in reality a lizard, not a frog or a toad, and its "horns" are actually spiny scales. Besides being the mascot of TCU, it is Texas's state reptile.

### 5. AKRON ZIPS

The University of Akron's nickname was first the Zippers, the result of a fan contest to name the school's athletic teams. Yes, somehow, Zippers was the winning entry! They were named after the Zipper, a rubber boot. As if that wasn't bad enough, the nickname was shortened to Zips in 1950. It's hard to imagine which is worse. If you're an athlete, do you really want to play for a team called the Zips? Didn't think so.

TEXAS CHRISTIAN UNVERSITY

Texas Christian University's SuperFrog mugs for the camera.

## 6. SAM HOUSTON STATE BEARKATS

Here's one I can't quite figure. For more than eighty years, Sam Houston State, an institution of higher learning, has called their athletic teams the Bearkats. That's right—kat with a "K". The name supposedly traced back to the old expression, "tough as a bearkat." And since the beast of the expression is supposed to be mythical, the school reasons there's no need to spell "Bearcat" correctly. I wonder if they spell everything correctly on their diplomas?

## 7. PURDUE BOILERMAKERS

No, the Boilermakers are not named after a drink, but they do have the largest mascot of any college athletic team. Purdue gets its nickname from The Boilermaker Special, a replica of a Victorian-era locomotive.

## 8. SOUTHEASTERN OKLAHOMA SAVAGES

Savages? Are they serious? When you think about the image you want for your university, Savage is the nickname you want associated with it? At least they can say it's unique. Unlike nicknames like Tigers and Wildcats, which are both shared by many universities, no one else can lay claim to the Savages nickname.

## 9. IDAHO VANDALS

From *Webster*'s—Vandal: n. one who willfully or ignorantly destroys, defaces, or damages property belonging to another or to the public. This definition sure didn't stop the University of Idaho in its search for a school nickname. It's not as bad as Savages, but it's pretty low. Idaho is the home of the potato. Why not something like the Spuds, or the Taters? Okay, those would be pretty lame, too, but they're better than what they have now.

## 10. DARTMOUTH BIG GREEN AND CORNELL BIG RED

These nicknames are not weird, nor are they outrageous. They're not offensive and they're not scary. They're just boring. I thought the Ivy League was supposed to be the best in higher education in America. Maybe it is, but not when it comes to school nicknames. I mean, the Big Green and the

Big Red? They couldn't come up with anything else? I'd include the Harvard Crimson on this list, but at least they don't have the ridiculous "Big" in their nickname, and Crimson is a little more descriptive than the plain old Red and Green.

# Don't Want to See Him Again

"**O**h, no, not him again." How many times have fans uttered those words about an opposing player? There are players and coaches who seem to be a thorn in the side of specific opponents. Here are ten men and the teams they tormented.

## 1. RANDY MOSS VERSUS THE COWBOYS

In Randy Moss's first three seasons, his Minnesota Vikings took on the Dallas Cowboys, and no matter how the Cowboys covered Moss, they couldn't stop him. On Thanksgiving Day of his rookie year in 1998, Moss caught just three passes against Dallas, but they were all good for touchdowns and 163 yards as the Vikings won 46–36. The next two times the teams met it was much the same. Moss caught thirteen balls combined with four more touchdowns. Then, in 2004, Moss caught two more touchdowns against Dallas, making it nine touchdowns in four games against the Cowboys.

## 2. JAMAL LEWIS VERSUS THE BROWNS

In the Ravens' Super Bowl championship season of 2000, rookie Jamal Lewis had a great game late in the season, rushing for 170 yards against division rival Cleveland. That was the start of a fabulous career against the Browns. After missing 2001 with an injury, Lewis was back the following season, twice rushing for more than 100 yards against the Browns, including a 187-yard, 2-touchdown outing. Then, in week two of 2003, after bragging to Browns defensive backs that he'd set a single-game record against them, he went out and did just that, gaining 295 yards on thirty carries. If that wasn't enough, in their second meeting he ran for another 205, giving him a clean 500 for two games.

### 3. DAN MARINO VERSUS THE JETS

Dan Marino had good numbers versus just about everybody, but he always seemed to have a little something extra up his sleeve when he played the Jets. Over the course of his career he posted a record of 17–13 record against them, but those seventeen wins are the second-most for any quarterback against another opponent, next to Marino's twenty-two versus the Colts. But against the Jets, Marino threw for more yards and touchdowns than any other team. And did he ever have big moments against Gang Green: In 1985 he hit Mark Duper for a last-minute touchdown bomb that helped Miami win the AFC Central; in 1986 he threw six touchdown passes in a 51–45 loss, but then came back in the second meeting to beat the Jets 45–3; and who could forget the infamous "fake spike" touchdown pass to Mark Ingram in 1994 that gave the Dolphins a win in a game in which they trailed by 18 points.

### 4. BOB GRIESE AND THE DOLPHINS VERSUS THE BILLS

When a Buffalo Bills fan thinks back to the 1970s, he or she may think of KISS, ABBA, maybe *Saturday Night Fever*, or the Bee Gees. But you know what else they remember from the 1970s? Their team never beat the Dolphins. That's right, zero for the 1970s. From a 28–3 win in Buffalo in their final meeting of 1969 until a 17–7 triumph in their first matchup in 1980, the Bills were an unbelievable 0–20 against their AFC East rival.

### 5. JOHN ELWAY VERSUS CLEVELAND

It all started with The Drive. The Cleveland Browns made three trips to the AFC Championship Game in the 1980s, but they never hit Super Bowl paydirt. Each time they got that far, John Elway and the Broncos were waiting for them. Elway's precision 98-yard drive in the 1986 title game helped Denver erase a late 20–13 deficit on their way to a 23–20 overtime win. In the 1987 and 1989 championship games, Elway guided the Broncos to big early leads en route to 38–33 and 37–21 victories. If it's any consolation to Browns fans, at least Elway and the Broncos got thumped in all three Super Bowls.

### 6. DERRICK THOMAS VERSUS SEATTLE

Some linebackers would be thrilled to record seven sacks in a season, so imagine how the Chiefs' Derrick Thomas felt in a 1990 game against the Seahawks at Arrowhead Stadium. From his right outside linebacker position, Thomas tormented Seattle quarterback Dave Krieg all afternoon, dropping him seven times to set an NFL single game record. But Thomas may have missed the biggest sack opportunity of the day on the final play from scrimmage. Thomas had Krieg in his sights, wrapped him up, but Krieg slithered away long enough to hit Paul Skansi with the winning touchdown in a 17–16 win.

### 7. LYNN SWANN VERSUS DALLAS

Cowboys fans get painful memories watching clips from Super Bowls X and XIII. Those were the two championship games that their team lost to the Pittsburgh Steelers, and the games in which Lynn Swann made himself a household name. In Super Bowl X Swann caught just four passes but still was named MVP. His receptions covered 161 yards and included a 64-yard touchdown that clinched the game late in the fourth quarter and a juggling 53-yard catch that has been at the top of NFL highlight reels for the last thirty years. Then, in Super Bowl XIII, a questionable pass interference call against Bennie Barnes while he covered Swann led to a Pittsburgh touchdown, Swann caught another touchdown to give the Steelers an insurmountable 18 point lead.

### 8. STEVE GROGAN VERSUS THE JETS

As quarterback for the New England Patriots, Steve Grogan got to see an awful lot of his AFC East rival New York Jets, and he was really happy to see them on the schedule in 1978 and 1979. In those two years, the Patriots were not a very hospitable host for the Jets. In 1978 they pounded them 55–21, and, as if that wasn't bad enough, Grogan and the Pats did them one better the following season—a 56–3 dismantling that is the worst loss in Jets franchise history.

### 9. JOHN ELWAY VERSUS MARTY SCHOTTENHEIMER

True, Schottenheimer was the coach of the Browns for two of their AFC Championship losses to Elway and the Broncos. But Marty gets his own entry here because Elway continued to haunt Marty in his next job with the Kansas City Chiefs. First, in 1992, Elway and the Broncos trailed the Chiefs by 13 points late in the fourth quarter, before he spun some magic and put two touchdowns on the board for a 20–19 win. That loss was the difference between a division title and a wild card berth for Kansas City. Then, in 1997, the Chiefs went 13–3 and had home field advantage throughout the playoffs, but Elway and the Broncos spoiled any chance at a Super Bowl with a 14–10 win in the divisional playoffs at Arrowhead Stadium.

## 10. BILL BELICHICK VERSUS PEYTON MANNING

Manning has had a brilliant career for the Colts, but he's never been able to solve the defenses of Bill Belichick's Patriots. Manning is just 1–7 against the Pats through 2004, including playoff losses in 2003 and 2004. Manning won again in 2005.

# Going Overtime

You hear coaches say it all the time: "Let's play our best football for sixty minutes." But there are occasions when sixty minutes isn't enough. Whether you want to call it "sudden death," or, as the great Curt Gowdy of NBC used to say, "sudden victory," overtime games can be some of the best the NFL has to offer. Here are some of the more remarkable overtime games in pro—and college—history.

## 1. BALTIMORE COLTS 23, NEW YORK GIANTS 17

The 1958 NFL Championship Game between the Colts and Giants at Yankee Stadium, widely regarded as the greatest NFL game ever played, was the first-ever overtime game. The Colts jumped out to a 14–3 lead in the second quarter, thanks to an Alan Ameche touchdown run and a 15-yard touchdown catch by Raymond Berry, but the Giants stormed back with two second-half touchdowns, the second of which, a 15-yard pass from Charlie Conerly to Frank Gifford, gave them a 17–14 lead. But John Unitas got things going again for the Colts, leading his team downfield for Steve Myhra's game-tying 20-yard field goal, which would send the game . . . where? Viewers at home, even fans in the stands, didn't know what would happen next. For the first time, overtime would decide an NFL game, and the first team to score would be victorious. Unitas then led the Colts downfield in overtime, where Ameche's second touchdown of the game, from the 1-yard line, gave the Colts the championship.

## 2. SAN DIEGO CHARGERS 41, MIAMI DOLPHINS 38

A beautiful early evening at the Orange Bowl was the setting for one of the most remarkable games in NFL history, a 1981 playoff matchup between San Diego and Miami. Dan Fouts and the Chargers took on the Dolphins, and with a little help from a Wes Chandler touchdown on a punt return, the Chargers jumped out to a 24–0 second quarter lead. However, Miami refused to fold.

Veteran quarterback Don Strock led the comeback, which included a perfectly executed hook and lateral play that running back Tony Nathan converted into a touchdown on the final play of the first half, cutting the San Diego lead to 24–17. A Strock touchdown pass tied the game in the third quarter, then the teams traded touchdowns before a Nathan touchdown gave Miami its first lead at 38–31. Fouts brought San Diego back, and his touchdown pass to James Brooks, which looked like it was intended for Kellen Winslow, made it 38–38. The Dolphins had a chance to win it in regulation, but Winslow blocked Uwe Von Schamann's field goal attempt. In overtime, with exhaustion evident on the faces of many players, both teams had field goal chances to win the game, but San Diego's Rolf Benirschke missed a short attempt, and Von Schamann had another opportunity blocked. Finally, Benirschke redeemed himself from 29 yards out to win it for the Chargers. The true star of the game was Winslow who, in addition to his blocked kick, caught thirteen passes for 166 yards and a touchdown.

### 3. **MIAMI DOLPHINS 27, KANSAS CITY CHIEFS 24**

As the American public settled in for their Christmas dinners, the Chiefs and Dolphins were settling into the longest game in NFL history. The 1971 game, played in Kansas City, was a classic back and forth affair. The Chiefs would grab a lead, then the Dolphins would tie it. A late touchdown by Miami tied the game at twenty-four, before Kansas City's Ed Podolak (who accounted for more than 300 total yards in the game) returned the ensuing kickoff 78 yards to the Miami 22. A trip to the AFC Championship Game against Baltimore hung in the balance as Jan Stenerud attempted a 31-yard field goal. But the usually reliable Stenerud missed, forcing overtime

Both teams had chances to score in the first overtime, but Stenerud had a 42-yard attempt blocked by Nick Buonoconti, and the Dolphins' Garo Yepremian missed a 52-yarder. Finally, after eighty-two minutes and forty seconds, Yepremian's 37-yard field goal won it for Miami, propelling them to three straight Super Bowl appearances, while the Chiefs would not play in the postseason for another fifteen years.

### 4. **OAKLAND RAIDERS 37, BALTIMORE COLTS 31**

In 1977, for the third consecutive year, the Colts faced the defending Super Bowl champion in the playoffs (after re-sounding losses to the Steelers in the previous two postseasons). But this game was much more competitive. Thanks to a 61-yard interception return for a touchdown by Bruce Laird, and Marshall Johnson's 87-yard kickoff return for a touchdown, the Colts kept it close and then took a 31–28 lead with two minutes left on a 13-yard run by Ron Lee. But Raiders quarterback Ken Stabler led his team downfield against a frenetic Colts defense and a boisterous crowd. Stabler launched a bomb to tight end Dave Casper (a play called the "Ghost to the Post") that set up a 22-yard field goal by Errol Mann to send the game to overtime. After trading a few possessions, the Raiders began a march deep into Colts territory. Stabler's 10-yard touchdown to Casper (his third of the game) in the second overtime sent the Raiders to the AFC Championship Game for the fifth consecutive year.

### 5. GREEN BAY PACKERS 12, CHICAGO BEARS 6

The 1980 season started splendidly for the Packers. In week one at Lambeau Field they were locked in a 6–6 overtime battle with the Bears. A drive deep into Chicago territory set them up for a game-winning field goal attempt by Chester Marcol, but Bears lineman Alan Page (yes, the same Alan Page of Purple People Eaters fame) made penetration and blocked the attempt. In one of the more fortuitous bounces in NFL history, the ball skipped right back to Marcol. The less-than-fleet kicker scampered 24 yards down the sideline for the winning points in an unlikely 12–6 win.

### 6. CAROLINA PANTHERS 29, ST. LOUIS RAMS 23

In a 2002 NFC divisional playoff matchup at the Edward Jones Dome in St. Louis, the Rams trailed Carolina by eleven points in the fourth quarter. That's when the Rams started to rally. A 1-yard touchdown by Marshall Faulk and a 2-point conversion cut the lead to three, and a successful onside kick gave the Rams the ball back. Despite a deep march into Carolina territory, the Rams played for the tie and got it when Jeff Wilkins converted a 33-yard field goal. In overtime both teams squandered opportunities, as Carolina kicker Jon Kasay missed from 45 yards and Wilkins came up short from 52. On the Rams's next possession, Ricky Manning picked off Marc Bulger at the Carolina 35-yard line.

Three plays later, on the first play of the second overtime,

Carolina quarterback Jake Delhomme hit wide receiver Steve Smith on a seam route near midfield. Smith split two defensive backs and outran the rest of the secondary to complete a spectacular 69-yard catch and run that sent the Panthers to the NFC Championship Game.

### 7. **ARKANSAS 58, OLE MISS 56**
In the longest college football game to date, the Razorbacks and Rebels finished regulation time of their 2001 contest tied at seventeen. From there, the game went on, and on, and on—for seven overtimes. Ole Miss quarterback Eli Manning threw for six touchdowns in the game, and Arkansas had three backs rush for more than 100 yards: Fred Talley, Mike Jones, and Cedric Cobb. The game ended only when Manning and Ole Miss were unable to complete a 2-point conversion that would have sent the game to overtime number eight.

### 8. **ARKANSAS 71, KENTUCKY 63**
What's with the Razorbacks and these long games? In 2003, Arkansas engaged in another classic, this time against Kentucky in Lexington. Tied at 24 at the end of regulation, the teams traded scores for the first six overtimes, as late afternoon faded into evening. Kentucky quarterback Jared Lorenzen had two touchdown passes and rushed for three more to pace the Wildcats. But on the first play of overtime number seven, Arkansas's Delori Birmingham ran twenty-five yards for the winning score. The Razorbacks held on defense, and escaped with a wild 71–63 win.

### 9. **NEW YORK JETS 26, NEW YORK GIANTS 20**
The first regular season game won in sudden death came in week eight of the 1974 season (there had been an earlier overtime game that season between Pittsburgh and Denver

but they finished in a tie), in a battle of New York City that was played in New Haven. Yes, in 1974 the Giants played their home games at Yale Bowl, following the closing of the old Yankee Stadium and while Giants Stadium was still under construction. The Giants led late in regulation, but the Jets tied it on a gutsy call by quarterback Joe Namath. Facing a fourth and goal, the gimpy Namath ran a naked bootleg, fooling everyone including some of his own teammates, and limped into the end zone to send the game to overtime. In overtime, following a missed field goal attempt by the Giants' Pete Gogolak, Namath drove the Jets to the win, connecting with running back Emerson Boozer on a 5-yard touchdown pass. It started the Jets on a season-ending six-game winning streak.

## 10. **DENVER BRONCOS 23, CLEVELAND BROWNS 20**

The Browns, looking for their first-ever Super Bowl appearance, hosted the Denver Broncos in the 1986 AFC Championship Game. Played on a sloppy track, the Browns took a 20–13 lead with five minutes left, as quarterback Bernie Kosar hit Brian Brennan with a 48-yard touchdown pass. That set the stage for "The Drive," as Denver quarterback John Elway led the Broncos on a scintillating 98-yard drive, capped by a 5-yard bullet touchdown pass to wide receiver Mark Jackson. In the overtime, the Broncos held on their first defensive possession, and when they got the ball for the first time, Elway drove them into field goal range. Rich Karlis sent the Broncos to Super Bowl XXI when he barely snuck a 33-yard field goal inside the left upright.

# Lighting up the Scoreboard

On more than a few occasions, the official scorekeeper has been really busy. Here are some of the highest scoring games in NFL history.

### 1. CHICAGO BEARS 73, WASHINGTON REDSKINS 0

The Bears and Redskins squared off for the 1940 NFL championship in Washington, and it was over so fast the Redskins never knew what hit them. Chicago coach George Halas unleashed his new "T" formation offense, and Hall of Fame quarterback Sid Luckman ran it to perfection. On the first series of the game, fullback Bill Osmanski busted loose for a 68-yard score, and the Bears were on their way. In all, the Bears picked off eight Redskins passes, rushed for an astounding 382 yards, and had eleven different men score touchdowns.

### 2. WASHINGTON REDSKINS 72, NEW YORK GIANTS 41

The Giants were in the midst of a miserable 1966 season, one in which they would win only a single game. In late November they traveled to Washington, where the Redskins blew their doors off, much to the delight of former Giant and then-Redskin Sam Huff, who had been let go by New York a couple of seasons earlier. Sonny Jurgensen led the way for the Redskins with three touchdown passes, including a 74-yarder to Charlie Taylor, and defensive back Brig Owens scored two touchdowns, one on a 62-yard fumble recovery and another on a 60-yard interception return. The 113 combined points is an NFL record for a single game.

### 3. CINCINNATI BENGALS 58, CLEVELAND BROWNS 48

In a 2004 matchup at Paul Brown Stadium in Cincinnati, the Bengals avenged an earlier defeat to the Browns in the second-highest scoring game in league history. Deltha O'Neal's interception return for a touchdown with fewer than two minutes left iced the game for Cincinnati, spoiling Kelly Holcomb's attempt at a remarkable comeback win. Holcomb threw for more than 400 yards and 5 touchdowns, including a 1-yarder to Steve Heiden to give the Browns a 48–44 lead with ten minutes remaining. But Rudi Johnson rushed for more than 200 yards for the Bengals, and Carson Palmer tossed four touchdown passes.

### 4. LOS ANGELES RAMS 70, BALTIMORE COLTS 27

In an October 1950 tangle at the Los Angeles Coliseum, the Rams became the first team to score 70 points in a regular season game. Eight Rams scored touchdowns, including Hall of Famers Tom Fears and Elroy "Crazylegs" Hirsch, and Hall of Fame quarterbacks Norm Van Brocklin and Bob Waterfield each tossed two touchdown passes. The Rams put up 21 points in both the first and fourth quarters.

### 5. NEW YORK JETS 62, TAMPA BAY BUCCANEERS 28

The Jets set a team record for points on a chilly November afternoon at the Meadowlands in 1985, but there was a history between the two teams that dated back to the previous season. The Jets and Bucs met in the final game of the 1984 season in Tampa Bay. Tampa Bay running back James Wilder was closing in on the all-time record for total yards from scrimmage in a single season, and head coach John McKay, with his team well ahead in the fourth quarter, ordered his defense to allow the Jets to score to give Wilder another crack at the record. Well, the defense did its part, but Wilder did not get the record, and the Bucs won 41–21. The Jets didn't forget what happened. Ken O'Brien threw five touchdown passes in the 1985 contest, including three to tight end Mickey Shuler.

### 6. ATLANTA FALCONS 62, NEW ORLEANS SAINTS 7

How's this for a way to start your season? A bright, sunny September day at Tulane Stadium, a big crowd for opening day, and the usually dreadful Falcons coming to town—the perfect recipe to get off on the right foot, correct? Well, not in 1973, as the Falcons jumped all over the Saints in a 62–7 win. The immortal Dick Shinner had three touchdown passes and Nick Mike-Mayer added two field goals for Atlanta. The momentum didn't exactly carry over for the Falcons: They lost their next three games and scored just 15 total points.

### 7. PHILADELPHIA EAGLES 64, CINCINNATI REDS 0

The largest shutout in regular-season NFL history belongs to the Eagles, who put a 64–0 goose egg on the old Cincinnati Reds in a November 1934 game in Philadelphia. Unfortunately for the Reds, this result was not uncommon in 1934. They finished 0–8 and were outscored 234–10 for the season.

### 8. SAN FRANCISCO 49ERS 56, ATLANTA FALCONS 17

In 1991 the Falcons went 10–6 to earn the final wild card berth in the NFC. During that season, Atlanta had a 6–0 record against teams from California, beating division rivals San Francisco and the Los Angeles Rams two times each, while also knocking off the Chargers and Raiders of the AFC. Head Coach Jerry Glanville then proclaimed that his Falcons were the "California State Champions" and made his team a makeshift trophy. The 49ers, they of four Super Bowl rings at the time, were not amused. The following season in Candlestick Park, Jerry Rice and Ricky Watters each scored three touchdowns, and the 49ers demolished the Falcons 56–17.

## 9. JACKSONVILLE JAGUARS 62, MIAMI DOLPHINS 7

The final game of Dan Marino's glorious career is one he— and anyone associated with the Dolphins—would like to forget. After finishing the 1999 regular season 14–2, Jacksonville earned home field advantage throughout the playoffs, and they put it to use early and often in the divisional round. The Jaguars jumped out to a 41–0 lead in the first half, which included a fumble return for a touchdown by defensive end Tony Brackens, and they never looked back. Jacksonville's 62 points and 55-point victory margin are second only to the Bears' 73-point romp over the Redskins in postseason history.

## 10. GREEN BAY PACKERS 48, WASHINGTON REDSKINS 47

In 1983 the Packers and Redskins combined for the highest scoring game in Monday Night Football history. The game featured more than 1,000 yards of offense and seventeen scores as the teams went back and forth the entire game. A 5-yard touchdown pass from Joe Theismann to Joe Washington gave the Redskins a 47–45 lead with three minutes to play. But Jan Stenerud gave the Pack the lead at 48–47 on a 20-yard field goal with just less than a minute to go. The Redskins again moved into scoring position, but Mark Moseley missed a 39-yard field goal attempt at the final gun. It was one of only two games the Redskins would lose all season—both were on Monday night and both were by 1 point (the other a was 31–30 loss to Dallas in week one).

# There's No Place Like Home

Every team likes to have the home field advantage. They have their own fans and they know all the intricacies of the place, like which way the wind blows. But what happens when the home field is unavailable and teams must play their "home" games somewhere else? Here are ten alternate fields and how teams fared in their home away from home.

## 1. CHICAGO STADIUM

Surely the strangest venue for an NFL game, Chicago Stadium, best known at the time as a venue for circuses, was home for the 1932 NFL Championship Game between the Chicago Bears and the Portsmouth Spartans. With a major snowstorm and a frigid cold front moving through Chicago, Bears coach George Halas, wary of a small turn out at Wrigley Field, proposed to move the game indoors, to Chicago Stadium. The field was not close to regulation size, stretching only 80 yards long and was about 15 yards short in width, and the offenses had trouble adapting. The game went scoreless for three quarters before Bronko Nagurski hit Red Grange with a touchdown pass on a fourth and goal from the 2-yard line. The Bears defense added a safety late in a 9–0 victory. It was the only NFL game played indoors before the opening of the Houston Astrodome.

## 2. COUNTY STADIUM

The Green Bay Packers have one of the best home field advantages in football when they play at Lambeau Field. But for forty-two years, from 1953 through 1994, the Packers played three home games a year a few hours away at Milwaukee's County Stadium (from 1938 through 1952 they played in Milwaukee's Marquette Stadium). Their record at County Stadium was 75–46–4 in the regular season, and 1–0 in the postseason—a 28–7 romp over the Rams in 1967.

## 3. MEMORIAL STADIUM (UNIVERSITY OF ILLINOIS)

In 2001 the Bears were the surprise team of the NFL. The final season at old Soldier Field saw Chicago finish with a 13–3 record and an NFC Central title. So hopes were very high for the 2002 season—one in which the Bears would be playing their home games 150 miles outside Chicago, in Champaign, at the University of Illinois' Memorial Stadium, while Soldier Field was renovated in the Windy City. But things soured quickly after a 2–0 start as the Bears, who basically had to travel to every game on their schedule, collapsed to a 4–12 finish. They finished up 3–5 in Champaign, including a late season win that put a severe crimp on the New York Jets's postseason plans.

## 4. YALE BOWL

During the 1973 and 1974 seasons, the New York Giants played their home games an hour north of the city in New Haven's Yale Bowl. Yankee Stadium, the Giants' home since 1956, was being renovated, and the Giants' new home in New Jersey's Meadowlands would not be ready until 1976, so the Giants were forced to play their final five games of 1973 and all of 1974 at Yale. And after two years there, were the Giants ever looking for their own home. In twelve games, they lost eleven. They didn't fare much better in 1975, either, when they called New York's Shea Stadium home. They were only 2–5 there.

## 5. HUSKY STADIUM

The Seattle Seahawks played in the Kingdome from their inception in 1976 through the 1999 season, but before moving into their new home, they played two years in Husky Stadium, the home of the University of Washington. They posted a 9–7 record there, but it was not the first time that they had to use Husky Stadium. In 1994 structural problems at the Kingdome played havoc on both the Seahawks and Major League Baseball's Mariners. The Seahawks were forced to play their first three games at Washington, posting a 1–2 record.

## 6. MEMORIAL STADIUM, UNIVERSITY OF MINNESOTA

In 1969 the Minnesota Vikings were on their way to their first of four Super Bowl appearances. But they were not the only team in the Twin Cities enjoying a banner season. The Twins won the inaugural American League Western Division championship, and faced the East champion Baltimore Orioles in the League Championship Series. That set up a scheduling conflict, as the Vikings were scheduled to play the Packers at Metropolitan Stadium the same day as a Twins playoff game. So, to accommodate, the NFL game was moved to Memorial Stadium at the University of Minnesota, affectionately known as the Brick House. A U-shaped single level stadium with small bleachers and a scoreboard covering the open end, it had served as the home field for the Minnesota Gophers since

1924. In what would be the only NFL game ever played there, the Vikings knocked off the Packers 19–7.

### 7. LIBERTY BOWL, VANDERBILT STADIUM
The Houston Oilers/Tennessee Oilers/Tennessee Titans had to have set some kind of record by having four home facilities in four years from 1996 through 1999. The year 1996 was the final season for the Astrodome, as the Oilers were moving to Tennessee for the 1997 season. That was spent in Memphis's Liberty Bowl, where sparse crowds greeted the Oilers. Memphis had been snubbed earlier in an attempt at an expansion NFL franchise, and fans did not take well to being a one-season stopping post for a team that would eventually end up in Nashville. That did not bother the Oilers, who finished 6–2 in Memphis. The 1998 season found the now-Titans playing in Nashville, but not at the glitzy new Adelphia Coliseum, which would be their home in 1999. Instead, they played at the intimate Vanderbilt Stadium, where they went just 3–5.

### 8. BUSCH STADIUM
Owner Georgia Frontiere moved the Rams from Los Angeles to St. Louis following the 1994 season, where they would play in the lush new TransWorld (now Edward Jones) Dome. But the facility would not be ready for opening day 1995, so the Rams played their first four home games at Busch Stadium, which had not hosted a football game since the late 1980s when the Cardinals still called St. Louis home. The Rams liked it there just fine, going 3–1 at Busch. Unfortunately, they went only 4–8 combined everywhere else and finished the season 7–9.

## 9. STANFORD STADIUM

The earthquake that struck northern California in October 1989 not only wreaked havoc on the World Series between the A's and the Giants, but it also caused problems for the San Francisco 49ers. Their game with the Patriots was scheduled for just five days after the quake at Candlestick Park. As a precaution, the game was moved to Palo Alto, home of the Stanford Cardinal. The 49ers won the game 37–20, becoming the first team to play a regular season home game in a stadium in which they had earlier won a Super Bowl (San Francisco beat Miami in Super Bowl XIX in Stanford Stadium just five years earlier).

## 10. MEMORIAL STADIUM (CLEMSON)

The expansion Carolina Panthers spent 1995, their first season, playing home games in Clemson's Memorial Stadium, sometimes called "Death Valley," while Ericsson Stadium was being constructed in downtown Charlotte. The Panthers played well at Clemson, dropping their first two before winning five of their final six. Their 5–3 home mark helped them achieve a quite-respectable 7–9 overall record.

# Sparkling Comebacks

We all remember what Yankees great Yogi Berra said: "It ain't over til it's over." As we see from the following list, Yogi wasn't just referring to baseball.

### 1. NEVADA 56, WEBER STATE 49

In a 1991 game at Reno, Weber State jumped all over Nevada in the first half, building up a 42–7 lead at the break. Nevada turned to backup quarterback Chris Vargas, and they probably wondered what they had been waiting for. Vargas led the Wolfpack to seven touchdowns, and Nevada had a remarkable 56–49 win that stands as the greatest comeback in college football.

### 2. BUFFALO BILLS 41, HOUSTON OILERS 38

Frank Reich carved a name for himself in Buffalo history with his dramatics in bringing the Bills back from a 35–3 deficit early in the third quarter. Touchdown passes to Don Beebe (one) and Andre Reed (three) gave the Bills a lead in the fourth quarter of the 1992 AFC Wild Card Game. An Al Del Greco field goal tied the game for the Oilers to send the game into overtime, but Steve Christie won it with a 32-yard field goal in the extra session. The 32-point deficit is the largest to be overcome in NFL regular or postseason history.

### 3. MARYLAND 42, MIAMI (FLA.) 40

Eight years earlier, Frank Reich led another memorable comeback, this time from 31 points down. On a warm November afternoon at the Orange Bowl, the defending national champion Miami Hurricanes and first-year coach Jimmy Johnson dropped 31 first-half points on the Terps. At halftime Bobby Ross called on Reich to take over for the ineffective Stan Gelbaugh, and take over he did, leading Maryland to 42 second-half points, including three touchdown passes and one touchdown run. A Rick Badanjek touchdown gave the Terps an 8-point lead, but Bernie Kosar brought the Canes back with a last-minute touchdown drive. But after hitting Eddie Brown for the score, his 2-point attempt was knocked away. How did the Hurricanes respond to the loss? Well, they hosted Boston College and Doug Flutie in their next game. You may have heard how that one turned out.

### 4. SAN FRANCISCO 49ERS 39, NEW YORK GIANTS 38

In a 2002 first-round playoff game in San Francisco, the Giants were taking it to the 49ers. Late in the third quarter they led 35–14, when tight end Jeremy Shockey dropped a sure touchdown pass. It didn't seem like that big of a miscue at the time, and they settled for a Matt Bryant field goal to make it 38–14. That's when Jeff Garcia and Terrell Owens responded with two quick touchdowns, one on a pass from Garcia to Owens, and then a Garcia run. Following each score, Garcia hit Owens with a 2-point conversion pass. After a field goal brought the Niners within five points, Garcia hit Tai Streets with the game-winning score with just less than a minute remaining. The Giants had a chance to win it, but a botched snap on a field goal attempt (which led to a blown call by the officials that went against the Giants) sealed their fate.

### 5. AUBURN 17, ALABAMA 16

As rivalries go, you can't find many more heated than Alabama–Auburn. The 1972 season provided one of those games where both teams were nationally ranked, and the game lived up to the hype. Birmingham's Legion Field was the site for the matchup between the  number 2 Crimson Tide and the number 9 Tigers. With about five minutes remaining in the fourth quarter, the Tide had a seemingly insurmountable 16–3 lead and dreams of an unbeaten regular season. Then lightning struck—twice. Auburn's Bill Newton became a state hero, blocking two punts. Each of his blocks was recovered and run into the end zone for scores by teammate David Langer. Thanks to Newton's feat, Auburn won 17–16.

### 6. INDIANAPOLIS COLTS 38, TAMPA BAY BUCCANEERS 35

A 2003 Monday night in Raymond James Stadium saw the Colts overcome a 21-point deficit in the final four minutes. Ronde Barber's interception return for a touchdown gave Tampa Bay a 35–14 lead. But the Colts were getting the ball back. Maybe Barber would have been better off just sitting on the ball instead of running it back into the end zone. A 90-yard kickoff return by Brad Pyatt set the Colts up for a touchdown to cut the lead back to fourteen points, and after recovering an onside kick, Peyton Manning found an inexplicably wide open Marvin Harrison for the score that made it 35–28. After the Bucs recovered the next onside kick and the Colts forced a punt, Manning again found Harrison wide open with a 52-yard pass to the 6-yard line. A Ricky Williams touchdown tied it, and the Colts won it on a Mike Vanderjagt field goal in overtime.

### 7. SAN FRANCISCO 49ERS 38, NEW ORLEANS SAINTS 35

In 1980, before the dynasty, Joe Montana gave us all a little hint that he might be something special. During a meaningless December game at Candlestick Park, Archie Manning's three touchdown passes gave the Saints a 35–7 halftime lead over the Niners. But the second half was all San Francisco. Montana rushed for one touchdown and threw for two more, as the 49ers stormed back to tie the game in the fourth quarter. A Ray Wersching field goal in overtime gave San Francisco a 38–35 win. The 28-point deficit is the largest overcome in a regular season NFL game.

### 8. BUFFALO BILLS 37, INDIANAPOLIS COLTS 35

Just five seasons after their remarkable comeback against the Oilers in the playoffs, the Bills found themselves in another pickle. During a 1997 regular season game at home with the Colts, they trailed Indianapolis 26–0, thanks to a Marshall Faulk run to the endzone, a Jim Harbaugh touchdown pass, and four field goals by Cary Blanchard. A Bills touchdown and field goal cut the lead to ten at the half. After another Blanchard field goal in the fourth quarter, the lead was 29–16 with less than eleven minutes to go. A touchdown pass by Todd Collins and two scoring runs by Antowain Smith put Buffalo up 37–29. The Colts had one last chance after a Marvin Harrison touchdown, but they were unable to complete a 2-point conversion that would have tied the game.

### 9. ST. LOUIS CARDINALS 31, TAMPA BAY BUCCANEERS 28

Trailing 28–3 entering the fourth quarter of a 1987 game, the Cardinals stormed back in front of the home crowd at Busch Stadium. Neil Lomax's three touchdown passes and Al Noga's 23-yard fumble return accounted for 28 points to help earn St. Louis the 31–28 win.

## 10. DETROIT LIONS 31, BALTIMORE COLTS 27

In 1957 a young John Unitas tossed four touchdown passes in the first three quarters to help the Colts to a 27–3 lead over the Lions at Tiger Stadium. But a touchdown pass by Tobin Rote and two more by Bobby Layne gave the Lions a stunning 31–27 win. A couple of months later, the same Lions would overcome a 20-point deficit in a playoff win over the 49ers.

# Seeing Double

Through more than eighty years, there have been many pairs of brothers to play in the NFL, including famous siblings like the Mannings and the Sharpes. But the list of twin brothers in the NFL is much shorter, as the following list shows: There have been just ten sets of twins to take the field.

### 1. GENE AND TOM GOLSEN
The Golsens were the first-ever twins to play in the NFL, teaming up for the 1926 Louisville Colonels. Gene played running back and Tom offensive line for the Colonels. Gene played in only one game and Tom played in three that one season. The Golsens remain the only twins to play for the same team at the same time.

### 2. TIKI AND RONDE BARBER
The Barber twins broke into the NFL from the University of Virginia in 1997, and have enjoyed long, distinguished careers. Tiki has become the all-time leading rusher for the New York Giants, helping to lead them to three playoff berths and Super Bowl XXXV, while Ronde has been a fixture in the Tampa Bay Buccaneers secondary, making a key interception in the 2002 NFC Championship Game win over the

Eagles. That propelled the Bucs to the Super Bowl in which they defeated the Raiders.

### 3. RALEIGH AND REGGIE MCKENZIE

Raleigh McKenzie had a fifteen-year career (a record for any twin) as an offensive lineman with the Redskins, Eagles, Chargers, and Packers, and he won two Super Bowl rings with Washington. His brother Reggie was a five-year linebacker with the Raiders and 49ers.

### 4. RICH AND RON SAUL

The Saul brothers each played twelve-year careers in the NFL. Rich suited up for the Los Angeles Rams as an offensive lineman from 1970 through 1981. He was a vital cog on some very good Rams teams, including the team that went to Super Bowl XIII and lost to the Steelers. Ron was also an offensive lineman; he split his career between the Houston Oilers and the Washington Redskins.

### 5. HAL AND HERB SHOENER

The Shoeners were the second set of twins to play in the NFL, and each had a very short career, beginning in 1948. Hal played three seasons with the 49ers as a defensive end, while Herb, also a defensive end, lined up for the Redskins for two years.

### 6. MARK AND MIKE BELL

The Bells became more famous for what they did off the field than anything they did on it, when they both served time in prison for cocaine possession. Mark played defensive end for the Seahawks and Colts from 1979 through 1984. Mike played the same position with Kansas City between 1979 and 1991, but he had to sit out the 1986 season on suspension following his drug arrest.

## 7. PHIL AND PAUL TABOR
The Tabors had short careers in the late 1970s and early 1980s. Phil played defensive line with the Giants for four years, while Paul had just one year in the league, seeing action at guard and center with the Bears in 1980.

## 8. KEITH AND KERRY CASH
The Cash twins, tight ends out of the University of Texas, both played six seasons in the NFL, beginning in 1991. After one year with the Steelers, Keith played five seasons with the Chiefs, while Kerry suited up for three teams: Indianapolis, Oakland, and Chicago.

## 9. RICARDO AND DEVON MCDONALD
Ricardo McDonald spent eight years as a linebacker with the Bengals (from 1992 through 1997) and the Bears (in 1998 and 1999), so he retired without winning all that often. Devon played just four years (also as a linebacker), but he was on the Indianapolis team that made a surprise run to the 1995 AFC Championship Game.

## 10. KATO AND WASSWA SERWANGA
The Serwangas, both defensive backs, had short careers in the NFL. Kato spent three years with the Patriots beginning in 1998, and finished his career with one season in Washington. Wasswa played just two years in the league, with the 49ers in 1999 and the Vikings in 2000.

# More Football by the Numbers

H ere are ten more of football's numerical milestones.

### 1. **ZERO**

Here's a quick trivia question: Which was the last NFL team to go through the regular season without a win? If you guessed Tampa Bay in 1976, you're wrong. In 1982 the Baltimore Colts, led by that immortal duo of head coach Frank Kush and quarterback Mike Pagel, did not win a game in the strike-shortened season. They finished 0–8–1, with the tie coming against the Packers.

### 2. **THIRTY-FIVE**

Between 1994 and 1996, a fellow by the name of Rich Kotite was an NFL head coach for two different franchises. His final season was 1994, with the Eagles, and after starting the season 7–2, Kotite and the Eagles lost seven in a row to end the year. After being fired by Philly, Kotite went to the New York Jets, where he turned a bad situation into an unmitigated disaster. The Jets went just 4–28 over his two seasons, meaning that his record over his last thirty-nine games as a head coach he had thirty-five losses.

### 3. SIX

Since Division 1AA schools began playing for a national championship in 1978, Georgia Southern has won the most national championships, with six. They won three under Erk Russell, one behind Tim Stowers, and they were coached by Paul Johnson to the other two titles. A perennial power, Georgia Southern also made two other championship games.

### 4. EIGHTY-FIVE

When Jake Delhomme hooked up with Muhsin Muhammad on an 85-yard touchdown in the fourth quarter of Super Bowl XXXVIII, it gave the Panthers a short-lived lead. But it also set a Super Bowl record for longest completion, breaking the record of eighty-one, set by Brett Favre and Antonio Freeman in Super Bowl XXXI.

### 5. SIXTY-SEVEN

Before the 1989 season, college field goal kickers were allowed to use a tee on field goal attempts, which helped on longer tries. And the longest successful field goals (67 yards) occurred in 1977 and 1978, by three collegiate kickers: Joe Williams of Wichita State, Steve Little of Arkansas, and Russell Erxleben of Texas.

### 6. 22.5

Before the 2001 season, the NFL record for sacks in a season was held by former Jet Mark Gastineau, with twenty-two. Many of Gastineau's off-field antics made him a guy not well-liked by folks in NFL circles, and those people were simply overjoyed when it looked as though his record would fall in

2001. The Giants' Michael Strahan was having a monster season, and going into the final weekend he had 21.5 sacks. All he needed was one more to break the record; Gastineau was even on hand to witness the historic moment. The Giants' opponent was the Packers, whose quarterback, Brett Favre, was said to have a good off-field relationship with Strahan. As the game progressed, the Packers had a big lead, and Strahan was getting nowhere near Favre. But lo and behold—with just a few minutes to play in the game, Favre rolled out in Strahan's direction and just fell down, allowing Strahan to cover him with a sack. Strahan celebrated like he'd just won the Super Bowl, despite his team finishing a 7–9 season. A few things seemed apparent: Favre had taken a dive so Strahan could get the record; Strahan celebrated a little too much; and Gastineau handled the whole thing remarkably well. That's amazing in and of itself, because whenever there's an event and Gastineau shows the most class, it's a bad sign.

### 7. **4,007**
Many quarterbacks have thrown for more than 4,000 yards in a season, but Joe Namath of the Jets is the only one to have done it in a 14-game season. In 1967, while the Jets were still in the AFL, Namath tossed for 4,007 yards as the Jets went 8–5–1.

### 8. **TWENTY**
In forty years as the head coach at Penn State, legendary head coach Joe Paterno has guided the Nittany Lions to thirty-one bowl appearances. PSU has gone 20–10–1 in those bowl games, and the twenty wins are a record for Paterno.

### 9. **2,066**
In 1985 San Francisco 49ers running back Roger Craig

accomplished a remarkable feat. He accounted for more than 1,000 yards, both on the ground and on receptions. He had 214 rushes for 1,050 yards; on top of that he caught ninety-two passes out of the backfield for another 1,016, for a total of 2,066 yards. Marshall Faulk is the only other person to match Craig's heroics, accounting for 2,429 combined yards for the Rams in 1999.

## 10. TWENTY
Tom Landry of the Cowboys holds the NFL record for postseason wins by a head coach. The unflappable Landry, who won two Super Bowls in his thirty years behind the Dallas bench, won twenty games against sixteen losses.

# They're Playing For What?

We all know that the NHL champion plays for the Stanley Cup, and that the NFL champion is awarded the Vince Lombardi Trophy. But in college football, there are other prized objects to be won, especially in rivalry games. Why, there's the Peace Pipe (Bowling Green versus Toledo), the Beehive Boot (Utah versus BYU), and the Bayou Bucket (Houston versus Rice), just to name a few. Here are ten more.

### 1. THE LITTLE BROWN JUG
When coach Fielding Yost brought his powerhouse Michigan team north to play Minnesota in 1903, he was worried about his opponents sabotaging the Wolverines' water supply. Before the game he sent someone to buy a five-gallon jug, so he could bring his own water. The jug, neither little nor brown, was mistakenly left behind following the game, a 6–6 tie that snapped a 28-game winning streak by Michigan. And when Yost demanded that Minnesota officials return it, Minnesota athletic director L. J. Moore told him he'd have to win it back. And thus a tradition was born. Michigan has had many opportunities to win the Little Brown Jug, and they've taken advantage: The Wolverines hold a 62–22 series lead over the Gophers.

## 2. THE STANFORD AXE

Awarded annually to the winner of the Stanford–California football game, the Stanford Axe is an axe head on a plaque. Maybe it's not the prettiest thing, but it's a valuable commodity on both campuses. Since 1933, when the tradition of giving it to the winning team began, the Axe has been stolen seven times—three times by students from Cal, and the other four by Stanford undergrads.

## 3. THE OLD OAKEN BUCKET

More than a century old, the Bucket has, for the last eighty years, gone to the winner of the Purdue–Indiana football game.

So why a bucket? When the schools decided that it would be great to play for something every season, they had to find something suitable for two schools from Indiana. The decision was made to find an "old oaken bucket," and this one had a history dating back to before football had even been played— it was believed to have been used by Union soldiers during the Civil War.

PURDUE UNIVERISITY SPORTS INFORMATION

The Old Oaken Bucket goes to the winner of each year's rivalry game between Purdue and Indiana University

### 4. THE SHOT GLASS

This sounds like it should be right up everyone's alley. So how did Coast Guard and RPI come to play every year for a substandard size shot glass? Back in the 1930s, there was a postgame tradition between the two schools to gather on the field for a toast. The shot glass in question may or may not have come from an RPI class reunion, and because it's size was so unique, it was decided that it would go each year to the game's winner.

### 5. PAUL BUNYAN'S AXE

Here's the University of Minnesota making another appearance on this list. Despite the fact that the Gophers had been playing football against the Wisconsin Badgers since 1890, it was not until 1948 that they began competing for Paul Bunyan's Axe. The Axe carries the scores of each game since 1948, hand painted on both the shaft and axehead.

### 6. THE SHILLELAGH

Hey, surprise, it's another Big Ten team! And it's Purdue again! Since 1957, Purdue and Notre Dame have played for the Shillelagh trophy. The base of the trophy is adorned with small footballs with the winning team and scores of each game.

### 7. THE LITTLE BROWN STEIN

Montana and Idaho have been competing in football border wars since 1903, with Idaho having won fifty-five of the eighty-four games. Since 1938, the two teams have played for the Little Brown Stein.

### 8. THE OLD BRASS SPITTOON

Does it seem like every Big Ten game is played for a trophy? Beginning in 1950, Indiana and Michigan State started playing for the Old Brass Spittoon. The spittoon is believed to have come from an old Michigan trading post, and it is believed to have existed before both universities were founded. Since they've been playing for the Spittoon, Michigan State has gotten comfortable with it in their possession, having won it thirty-eight times.

### 9. THE GOLDEN EGG
Mississippi and Mississippi State play each season for the Golden Egg. It's actually a trophy of an old-time football and was called an egg because of its shape. They've played 102 times with Ole Miss holding a big advantage, 58–38–6.

### 10. THE SWEET SIOUX TOMAHAWK
It's only appropriate that we end the list with a couple more Big Ten teams, no? Illinois and their in-state rival Northwestern meet for the right to take home the Sweet Sioux Tomahawk. Originally, the teams played for a wooden Indian, similar to the one you'd see outside of a cigar store, but that ended when its size caused problems with transporting it. The Illini hold a 51–43–5 edge in the series.

# Wild!

In 1978 the NFL expanded its regular season from fourteen games to sixteen, and increased the number of playoff teams from eight to ten, to allow for one wild card game per conference. Subsequently, the league would add two more playoff teams in 1990. Befitting its name, wild things sometimes happen on Wild Card Weekend.

### 1. 1978 ATLANTA FALCONS 14, PHILADELPHIA EAGLES 13

On a gloomy afternoon at Fulton County Stadium, the Falcons and Eagles clashed in the first-ever wild card game following the 1978 season. The visitors controlled the game throughout, leading 13–0 midway through the fourth quarter, but that's when Steve Bartkowski rallied the hometown Falcons. He tossed two touchdowns in the final eight minutes, the second giving the Falcons a 14–13 lead. Philadelphia responded, as Ron Jaworski led the Eagles down the field, but rookie kicker Mike Michel missed a 34-yard field goal with just more than a minute left and Atlanta escaped with a win.

### 2. 1999 TENNESSEE TITANS 22, BUFFALO BILLS 16 (THE MUSIC CITY MIRACLE)

The Tennessee Titans had finished 1999, their inaugural

season at Adelphia Coliseum in Nashville, with a perfect 8–0 home record, and they looked to add to it on Wild Card Weekend. But it would not be easy, as their opponents were the 11–5 Buffalo Bills. In a tight, low scoring game, Al Del Greco gave the Titans the lead with a 36-yard field goal with just more than a minute remaining. But Rob Johnson and the Bills were not done. Johnson marched Buffalo right down the field, and Steve Christie's 41-yard field goal with seventeen seconds remaining appeared to give the Bills the victory. The Titans had one chance—a big kickoff return. To try and prevent just that, Christie launched a high, short kickoff that was fielded by up-back Lorenzo Neal, who handed the ball off to Frank Wycheck. Wycheck took a step right, then turned around completely to fire a lateral to Kevin Dyson on the left sideline. To the naked eye, it looked like an illegal forward pass, but replays showed it to be a legal play—barely. Dyson had a wall of blockers and went untouched down the sideline for the touchdown and a miraculous 22–16 win.

### 3. 1992 BUFFALO BILLS 41, HOUSTON OILERS 38 (THE MIRACLE AT RICH STADIUM)

In 1992 the Bills were in the playoffs for the fifth straight season, and they were looking for their third consecutive Super Bowl appearance. But they'd have to do it as wild cards, since Miami won the AFC East. The Bills entertained the Houston Oilers in the first round, and the game looked like it was over at halftime. Warren Moon was sensational, leading the Oilers on four touchdown drives, and after safety Bubba McDowell returned a Frank Reich interception for a touchdown, the Oilers led 35–3 two minutes into the third quarter. Then, like thunder, the comeback struck. Kenneth Davis punched in a 1-yard touchdown, and after Steve Christie recovered his own onside kick, Reich hit Don Beebe for a touchdown, and it was 35–17. It was three and out after that for Houston, and five plays later, Reich found Andre Reed for a 35-yard score. The lead was down to eleven, and the concern grew on the Oilers sideline. A couple of plays later, Moon was intercepted, and Reich and Reed connected again, making it a 35–31 game. The Bills four-touchdown onslaught took just seven minutes of game time. Late in the fourth quarter, Reich hooked up with Reed a third time, giving the Bills their first lead. Houston was able to force overtime with a late Al Del Greco field goal, but a Nate Odomes interception early in the extra session set up Christie's game-winning field goal, giving the Bills a remarkable 41–38 win.

### 4. 1993—GREEN BAY PACKERS 28, DETROIT LIONS 24

This was Brett Favre's welcome to the NFL Playoffs, and the Pontiac Silverdome crowd was hoping he would go home empty handed. The Lions had the lead, thanks in part to a Favre interception that was brought back for a score. But the Packers hung close, with a playoff record 101-yard interception return for a touchdown by George Teague a key play. Green Bay trailed 24–21 with under two minutes to play when Favre gave the fans a taste of his magic. Scrambling out of the pocket, he planted and threw a bomb to an inexplicably wide open Sterling Sharpe, giving the Packers the win and the Lions another painful postseason loss.

### 5. 2002—ATLANTA FALCONS 27, GREEN BAY PACKERS 7

Nine years after Favre's heroics, he got a taste of his own medicine when another hot-shot young quarterback walked into his building—Lambeau Field—and came out with a victory. Few gave Michael Vick and the Falcons a shot in their wild card game against the Packers. After all, few dome teams have had success in cold-weather playoff games, and no road team had ever—ever!—won a playoff game at Green Bay. But

Vick drove Atlanta to an early score, and a touchdown on a blocked punt gave the Falcons a two-score edge. They wouldn't relinquish the lead from there, as they won 27–7.

### 6. 2004—NEW YORK JETS 20, SAN DIEGO 17

On a drizzly night at Qualcomm Stadium, the Jets had this game won, then lost, then finally won again, all inside ten minutes of game time. Fast forward to the fourth quarter. The Jets led 17–10, but the Chargers were driving against a tiring New York defense. San Diego reached the 1-yard line, when the Jets tightened. Facing a fourth and goal with the season on the line, Chargers quarterback Drew Brees dropped back to pass on a play fake. But the Jets read it perfectly, and blitzing linebacker Eric Barton was quickly in Brees's face. Brees's only hope was to throw up a prayer that fell incomplete. The game was over—but wait! Barton was flagged for roughing the passer with a vicious forearm he threw at Brees's head. With new life, Brees hit Antonio Gates for a touchdown on the next play, sending the game into overtime. On their first series of the overtime, the Chargers marched into Jets territory, but they got a little conservative and settled for a 40-yard field goal attempt by rookie Nate Kaeding. Kaeding missed, and the Jets drove down the field behind quarterback Chad Pennington and backup running back Lamont Jordan to set up Doug Brien's game winning 28-yard field goal.

### 7. 1990—MIAMI DOLPHINS 17, KANSAS CITY CHIEFS 16

In 1990 the Dolphins hosted a Chiefs team looking for its first postseason win since Super Bowl IV. Early in the fourth quarter, it looked like they were going to get it. The Chiefs led 16–3 and had held the potent Dolphins offense in check. But Dan Marino rallied the troops, and two short touchdown passes gave the Fish a 1-point lead. The Chiefs had time for a final drive and looked like they had advanced into field goal range. But a penalty on guard Dave Szott pushed Nick Lowery's game-winning attempt back to 52 yards, and the kick came up just short.

### 8. 1987—MINNESOTA VIKINGS 44, NEW ORLEANS SAINTS 10

By the 1987 season, the New Orleans Saints had been in existence for twenty-one years, and the city of New Orleans had hosted six Super Bowls. But the Saints had never played host to a playoff game. When it finally happened it looked like they weren't prepared for it, or like they had spent a little too much time celebrating on Bourbon Street, because Wade Wilson and the Vikings came marching into the Superdome and did a little dance on the home team. The Saints lost 44–10 and would not actually win a home playoff game until after the 2000(!) season.

### 9. 1996—JACKSONVILLE JAGUARS 30, BUFFALO BILLS 27

In 1996 the Bills were a proud, veteran team with a number of holdovers from their Super Bowl run of the early 1990s. The Jaguars were a second-year franchise that needed a furious late season run just to finish 9–7 and make the playoffs. Many thought it was a mismatch, but the feisty Jaguars and their young quarterback Mark Brunell kept the Bills at bay, pulling off the first of two major upsets (they would knock off the Broncos at Mile High a week later). It was the first time Buffalo had lost a playoff game at Rich Stadium.

### 10. 2003—GREEN BAY PACKERS 33, SEATTLE SEAHAWKS 27

The 2003 NFC Wild Card Game featured Seattle head coach Mike Holmgren facing the team he had led to a win in Super Bowl XXXI. The Seahawks trailed in the second half but battled back to tie the game behind quarterback (and former Packer) Matt Hasselbeck. With the game all even at the end of regulation, Hasselbeck was one of the captains to take the field for the overtime coin toss, and when the Seahawks won that toss, Hasselbeck yelled, "We want the ball, and we're gonna score." Problem was, a field microphone caught it, and the whole Lambeau Field crowd and a national television audience heard it. He did get his team close to midfield, but Green Bay cornerback Al Harris intercepted a sideline route and returned it 52 yards for the game-winning touchdown. It was the first time in NFL playoff history that a game was decided by an overtime touchdown by the defense.

# I Used to Be a Quarterback

Many times you hear players referred to as a "good college quarterback," only never to see them play a down in the NFL. These college QBs took a different path to the pros: They changed positions. Here are some of the better known one-time quarterbacks.

## 1. HINES WARD
During a collegiate career at Georgia, Ward was as versatile as they come. He excelled at the scatback position, at wide receiver, and he also made a name for himself calling signals as a sophomore, throwing for more than 900 yards as a Bulldog. He also had more than 1,000 yards rushing and receiving with Georgia. He was drafted by the Pittsburgh Steelers in 1998 as a wide receiver, and he's been to three Pro Bowls since he arrived in the Steel City.

## 2. ANTWAAN RANDLE EL
The Steelers must really like these college quarterbacks as wide receivers, because four years after they drafted Ward, they picked up Antwaan Randle El from Indiana. In a stellar

career with the Hoosiers, Randle El etched his name in the NCAA record book. He was the only Division 1A player to ever rush for more than 3,000 yards and pass for 7,000 yards in a career. Likewise, he's the only player to ever pass for forty touchdowns and score forty touchdowns. As a Steeler, Randle El notched 127 receptions in his first three seasons, and he also rushed for 243 yards.

### 3. NOLAN CROMWELL

In the 1970s and 1980s, Nolan Cromwell was a top defensive back for the Los Angeles Rams. In a twelve-year career, he played in 161 games and collected thirty-seven interceptions, and he was one of the anchors of the defense that led the Rams to eight playoff appearances. But before he went to L.A., Cromwell played his college ball at Kansas. Cromwell was a safety there as well, but coach Fred Moore switched his offense to a wishbone attack and installed the fleet Cromwell as his quarterback. In 1977 he was named Big 8 Male Athlete of the Year.

### 4. MARLON BRISCOE

Coming out of Omaha University, Marlon Briscoe was the AFL Rookie of the Year as a quarterback with the Denver Broncos, which was no small feat considering he was working against stereotypes as a black starting quarterback. "Marlon the Magician" only lasted a season with the Broncos, after which he tried to negotiate a pay raise and was shipped off to Buffalo, where he was turned into a wide receiver. He stuck around the league through the 1976 season, and along the way he picked up two Super Bowl rings with the Miami Dolphins.

### 5. PHIL BRADLEY

A quarterback during his college days at the University of

Missouri, Bradley was also a star baseball player, and he was taken in the third round of the 1981 draft by the Seattle Mariners. He spent eight years as an outfielder in the big leagues, batting .300 three times. In 1988 as a member of the Phillies, Bradley became the first player to hit a home run in a night game at Wrigley Field. However, the game was called on account of rain before it became official, so Bradley was never officially credited with the feat.

### 6. MARK MALONE

The ESPN analyst was a star quarterback at Arizona State and eventually went on to play quarterback in the NFL with the Steelers. His 99-yard touchdown run stands as the longest in Sun Devils history. But early in his pro career, Pittsburgh experimented with Malone at wide receiver, and in 1981 he set a franchise record when he hauled in a 91-yard touchdown pass from Terry Bradshaw.

### 7. SCOTT FROST

In 1997 Frost led the Nebraska Cornhuskers to an undefeated season and their third national championship in four years. His athleticism led Bill Parcells and the New York Jets to draft Frost in the third round of the 1998 draft—as a safety. Frost played a key role in the Jets nickel package as a rookie, when the Jets went 12–4 and won the AFC East. He lasted three seasons total in New York.

### 8. WOODY DANTZLER

He was a magician calling signals at Clemson, a one-man wrecking crew who all opposing coaches had to key on. During his career, he set fifty (fifty!) individual Clemson records and was a Heisman candidate as a senior. In 2003 he played for the Dallas Cowboys, where he functioned primarily as a return man. That was his only year in the NFL, but he made it

CLEMSON UNIVERSITY SPORTS INFORMATION

Clemson quarterback Woody Dantzler made the switch to kick returner in his short-lived NFL career memorable with one of the most exciting kick return touch-downs you'll ever see, against the 49ers.

### 9. JIM JENSEN

In two years as quarterback at Boston University, Jensen led the Terriers to seventeen wins, and his college career was capped with an appearance in the Senior Bowl. The exposure of the Senior Bowl helped him get drafted by the Miami Dolphins in the eleventh round of the 1981 draft. Jensen hung around twelve years in the NFL as a valuable special teams player, but as a receiver he was also a favorite target of Dan Marino. Jensen frequently lined up wide, or would go out of the backfield, as an effective third-down receiving option.

### 10. KORDELL STEWART

Had Stewart played a decade or so earlier, he may have switched positions coming out of the University of Colorado. But Kordell remained a quarterback through a number of tumultuous years with the Steelers, before moving on to the Bears in 2003 and the Ravens in 2004, as a backup to Kyle Boller. So why is he on this list? Well, in a 2004 game against the Jets, the Ravens were short a punter when Dave Zastudil was injured. Coach Brian Billick turned to Stewart, who came through. He punted five times for a respectable 35-yard average. His longest was 42 yards and he dropped two inside the 20.

# Thanksgiving Turkeys

A hh, Thanksgiving. Time to gather the family, toss a turkey and all the trimmings in the oven, and gather around
the television to watch some football. They've been playing
football on Thanksgiving almost as long as they've been stuff-
ing the big bird. Here are some of the more memorable Turkey Day moments, in chronological order.

1. **1925—CHICAGO BEARS 0, CHICAGO CARDINALS 0**
A crowd of 36,000 filled Wrigley Field to see Bears rookie
Red Grange, the "Galloping Ghost," take on the crosstown
rival Cardinals. The teams battled to a scoreless tie, but the
story of the day was the attendance—the largest to see an
NFL game at the time. Grange's popularity was enormous
thanks to his legendary career at the University of Illinois, and
the crowd was there mostly to see him.

2. **1929—CHICAGO CARDINALS 40, CHICAGO BEARS 6**
The Comiskey Park crowd saw the home team Cardinals back
Ernie Nevers make history with one of the greatest individual
performances of all time. The Hall of Famer rushed for six
touchdowns (still an NFL record) and converted four out of
six PATs, accounting for all forty of his team's points—the
NFL's longest standing individual record.

### 3. 1934—CHICAGO BEARS 19, DETROIT LIONS 16

Two holiday traditions were born in 1934: This was the inaugural Thanksgiving game in Detroit, the beginning of a relationship now in its seventh decade; and, perhaps more importantly, this was the first national network broadcast of an NFL game. Fans nationwide listened in on NBC radio as the Bears squeaked by the Lions at Tiger Stadium—oh my!

### 4. 1962—DETROIT LIONS 26, GREEN BAY PACKERS 14

Vince Lombardi's Packers were the NFL's best team in 1962, and they would go on to beat the Giants for the championship. They entered Detroit on Thanksgiving day without a loss, but they were given a rude welcome by the Lions defense. Led by Joe Schmidt and a young defensive coordinator named Don Shula, the Lions swarmed Green Bay quarterback Bart Starr all afternoon. Starr was sacked eleven times, and the Lions "D" got in on the scoring too, with a touchdown on a fumble return and a safety. Detroit led 26–0, before two late touchdowns made the score respectable.

### 5. 1971—NEBRASKA 35, OKLAHOMA 31

On a chilly Turkey Day, the two top college teams in America faced off in Norman, Oklahoma. The game between the Nebraska Cornhuskers and Oklahoma Sooners lives on as "The Game of the Century." There were many story lines to the game. Oklahoma's offense was the best in the nation, while defending national champion Nebraska was riding a 29-game winning streak. Both teams had Heisman Trophy candidates: Greg Pruitt of the Sooners, and the Cornhuskers' Johnny Rodgers. Following Rodgers's electrifying punt return for a touchdown in the early going, the game went back and forth, with the Sooners twice coming back from 11-point deficits to reclaim the lead—once at 17–14 and later at 31–28 (the only two times in the *season* that Nebraska trailed). The outcome was not decided until the final minutes, when Nebraska marched 74 yards for the winning score, a touchdown run by Jeff Kinney, his third TD of the game. The victory propelled Nebraska on to the Orange Bowl, where they would win their second consecutive national championship.

### 6. 1974—DALLAS COWBOYS 24, WASHINGTON REDSKINS 23

Things didn't look good for Dallas. The rival Redskins had marched into Texas Stadium and were putting a hurting on the Cowboys. In the third quarter Washington had built a 16–3 lead and had knocked Dallas quarterback Roger Staubach out of the game. Enter Clint Longley. The Dallas rookie came on to spark his team with three late touchdowns, the final score with just twenty-eight seconds remaining in the game. He found Drew Pearson wide open behind the Washington secondary for a 50-yard touchdown and a 24–23 win.

### 7. 1976—DETROIT LIONS 27, BUFFALO BILLS 14

A capacity crowd at the Pontiac Silverdome got a double holiday treat. The Lions cruised to an easy 27–14 win over the Bills, while the Bills' O.J. Simpson set a then-NFL record by rushing for 273 yards.

### 8. 1993—MIAMI DOLPHINS 16, DALLAS COWBOYS 14

The Cowboys breathed a sigh of relief. On the snow-covered turf of Texas Stadium, Jimmie Jones had blocked a game-winning field goal attempt by Miami's Pete Stoyanovich with only seconds remaining. As the ball rolled harmlessly toward the goal line, all Dallas had to do was let the ball roll dead and they would walk away with a win. But one Cowboy couldn't help himself. He slid the ball, allowing Miami to recover with three seconds left—enough time for Stoyanovich to knock home the game-winner. Who committed the gaffe? As NBC analyst Bob Trumpy said, "Oh no, it's Leon Lett." You'll recall that just ten months earlier, Lett had committed another big blunder in Super Bowl XXVII, getting stripped of the ball by Buffalo's Don Beebe as he was about to cross the goal line with a touchdown.

### 9. 1998—DETROIT LIONS 19, PITTSBURGH STEELERS 16

The Lions roared back from a 10-point deficit to force overtime against the Steelers. Then things really got interesting. As the captains for the two squads gathered at midfield for the overtime coin toss, referee Phil Luckett grabbed the NFL coin. As they are always instructed, the opposing team called the flip in the air. Pittsburgh's Jerome Bettis can clearly be heard calling "tails." When Luckett announced that it was a tail, he turned to the Lions, and said the Steelers had called "heads." That did not sit well with Bettis or Pittsburgh coach Bill Cowher, who argued vehemently to no avail. The Lions took the overtime kickoff and marched down the field for a game-winning Jason Hanson field goal.

### 10. 2004—INDIANAPOLIS COLTS 41, DETROIT LIONS 9

The Lions had the misfortune to take on Peyton Manning and the Colts when Manning was in the midst of the hottest streak of his career. On the way to a record forty-nine touchdown passes in 2004, Manning had a huge day at Ford Field, tossing three touchdown passes to Marvin Harrison, and another three to Brandon Stokley. With their 41–9 win, the Colts had a lot to celebrate that day.

# Full Of Grace

Football's most exhilarating, most heartbreaking play is the last-second touchdown pass that snatches victory from the jaws of defeat—the Hail Mary. The Hail Mary pass has given us some of the most incredible finishes on both the pro and college gridiron—and hopefully this list will bring the book to a remarkable finish.

## 1. ROGER STAUBACH

The phrase "Hail Mary" became part of the sports vernacular in 1975. The Dallas Cowboys trailed the Minnesota Vikings 14–10 in the fourth quarter of a divisional playoff game at Metropolitan Stadium. With time running out, and Dallas in possession at the 50-yard line, Cowboys quarterback Staubach hurled a bomb down the right sideline toward Drew Pearson, who was well covered by cornerback Nate Wright. The ball was slightly underthrown, and Pearson appeared to make contact with Wright at the 5-yard line. Wright fell down, and Pearson hauled the ball in and scampered into the end zone for the game-winning score. Safety Paul Krause arrived late in coverage and vociferously complained to the official that Pearson should have been called for offensive pass

interference. The Vikings ended their season in disappoint-
ment, while the win propelled the Cowboys on to the Super
Bowl.

## 2. DOUG FLUTIE

On the Friday after Thanksgiving in 1984, Bernie Kosar's
Miami Hurricanes and Doug Flutie's Boston College Eagles
put on a show for a national television audience, combining
for more than 1,100 yards of total offense and 92 points. But
the game is forever remembered for its wild finish. With twenty-
eight seconds left, Miami tailback Melvin Bratton scored from
three yards out to give the Hurricanes a 45–40 lead. Flutie
then led his offense on the field, with his team needing eighty
yards for a touchdown. Two completions brought the Eagles
to the Miami 48-yard-line, with just six seconds to play. With
time left for one play, Flutie rolled far to the right to allow his
receivers time to reach the end zone. He uncorked a long
spiral that went over the outstretched hands of the Miami secondary and dropped right into the arms of wide receiver Gerard
Phelan, who cradled the ball in the end zone and fell to the
Orange Bowl turf, where he was mobbed by teammates. Flutie
ended up winning the Heisman Trophy, and Boston College
would go on to defeat Houston in the Cotton Bowl.

## 3. KORDELL STEWART

In a 1994 early season matchup of college powers, the University of Colorado Buffaloes traveled to Ann Arbor to take
on the Michigan Wolverines. Michigan held a 26–14 lead in
the fourth quarter, before Colorado, behind their dynamic
quarterback Kordell Stewart, rallied back. After cutting the
lead to 5 points, Colorado was on the doorstep again, but
Stewart fumbled away a possible scoring chance right near
the goal line. When the Buffaloes got the ball back, it looked
as though they were too far away to finish their comeback.

With six seconds left on the clock, Colorado was on its own 36-yard line. Stewart rolled to his left back to the twenty-seven and let fly. The pass traveled 73 yards in the air, when it was tipped up in the air away from Michigan safety Chuck Winters by wideout Blake Anderson, and receiver Michael Westbrook soared in to scoop the ball out of the air and gave Colorado an unbelievable 27–26 win.

## 4. TOMMY KRAMER

On the next-to-last weekend of the 1980 season, the Minnesota Vikings needed a win at home against the Cleveland Browns to clinch a playoff spot. Midway through the fourth quarter the Vikings trailed 23–9, and things looked bleak. But then quarterback Tommy Kramer started a rally. Two touchdowns got them close, but a missed PAT by Rick Danmeier left them trailing by a point. Minnesota took possession one last time with twelve seconds remaining and the ball at their own 20-yard line. On first down, Kramer sent three wideouts deep down the right sideline, but fired a short pass over the middle to tight end Jim Senser, who executed a perfect hook and lateral to running back Ted Brown. Brown scampered all the way to the Cleveland forty-seven before stepping out of bounds with one second on the clock. With time left for one play, Minnesota's wide receivers raced down the right sideline toward the end zone, and Kramer hurled a bomb in that direction. Receiver Terry LeCount leaped along with three Cleveland defenders, and the ball tipped toward the goal line, where the Vikings' Ahmad Rashad hauled it in for a remarkable touchdown that clinched a 28–23 win and a playoff spot.

## 5. JIM MCMAHON

Jim McMahon was the quarterback for Lavell Edwards' high-octane offense at BYU, as they took on SMU in the 1980 Holiday Bowl in San Diego. The Cougars trailed 45–25 with less than three minutes to play, but that's when McMahon started to heat up. First he hit Matt Braga with a touchdown pass. After going for two and failing, BYU recovered an onside kick. McMahon completed two straight passes to put the Cougars on the 1-yard line, setting up a Scott Phillips touchdown run. Now, just 1:58 remained. SMU took over possession after recovering another onside kick. Their series stalled, and they had a punt blocked, on fourth down BYU had one last shot with thirteen seconds left and the ball at the SMU 41. After two incompletions, McMahon heaved a Hail Mary toward receiver Clay Brown, who grabbed it in the end zone, surrounded by three defenders. The extra point gave BYU an unlikely 46–45 victory.

## 6. MARCUS RANDALL

When LSU played Kentucky in Lexington in 2002, it looked like the Wildcats had pulled off a big win when Taylor Begley knocked home a 29-yard field goal with eleven seconds left, to give the Wildcats a 30–27 lead over the Tigers. The Kentucky crowd went wild. It looked like a combination of Kentucky Derby Day and a UK appearance in the Final Four, as the crowd surged out of the stands and circled the field. LSU quarterback Marcus Randall completed a short pass to the 25-yard line and called timeout with two seconds left. Kentucky players doused head coach Guy Morriss with a big bucket of Gatorade. With time for one play, Randall dropped back. As the play unfolded, jubilant Wildcat fans stormed the field and started tearing down a goalpost. Randall's pass reached the Kentucky 30-yard line, where it was tipped twice and caught in full stride by wideout Devery Henderson inside the 20. A diving attempt by cornerback Derrick Tatum went for naught, and Henderson scored, leaving an entire stadium in shock.

## 7. ZAK KUSTOK

In a 2000 game at the Metrodome (note that this is the third game on this list played in Minnesota), Northwestern trailed the Minnesota Golden Gophers 35–14 in the third quarter. Behind quarterback Zak Kustok, the Wildcats converted five fourth-downs in a furious rally to tie the game. At 35–35, it looked like the game was headed for overtime. But with just a few seconds remaining, Kustok heaved a ball into the right corner of the end zone, where it was tipped back toward the goal line into the hands of Sam Simmons. He cradled it, untouched, for the winning touchdown.

## 8. SCOTT FROST

Nebraska traveled to the University of Missouri in 1997 looking to preserve an undefeated season, but the Tigers proved to be a feisty foe. The Cornhuskers trailed 38–31 with just more than a minute to play, and they took over possession 67 yards from a tying touchdown. Quarterback Scott Frost led his team down the field to the Missouri twelve, but only seven seconds remained. Frost fired a bullet that hit Shevin Wiggins right in the numbers, but he was well covered and the ball was tipped down toward Wiggins' feet. Wiggins flipped it over his head with his foot, and Matt Davidson grabbed it for a touchdown before it hit the turf. Wiggins later claimed that he kicked it on purpose, though it's hard to believe that he would know that Davidson would be in the vicinity. Nebraska won the game 45–38 in overtime on a Frost touchdown run, and then went on to their third national championship in four years, sharing it with Michigan.

## 9. STEVE BARTKOWSKI

Atlanta Falcons quarterback Steve Bartkowski enters this list for not one, but two game-winning Hail Mary passes from his career. First, in 1978, the Falcons trailed the Saints 17–6 late in the fourth quarter. Following an 80-yard touchdown drive, Atlanta trailed 17–13 with less than a minute to play. With nineteen seconds left, Bartkowski hurled a 59-yard pass down the sideline, where it was tipped to Alfred Jackson, who scored the touchdown that silenced the Superdome. Then, in 1983, his pass to Billy "White Shoes" Johnson answered the prayers of the home folks, as the Falcons pulled out an incredible 28–24 win over the San Francisco 49ers.

## 10. BILLY JOE TOLLIVER

Remarkably, eight seasons after Johnson's catch, the Falcons and 49ers were involved in a Hail Mary game on the same field. With nine seconds left and the 49ers up 14–10 (San Francisco had just scored with less than a minute to play), Tolliver, in for the injured Chris Miller, tossed a 44-yard touchdown pass to Michael Haynes, who pulled the ball out of a crowd. The 17–14 Falcons' win was their second of the season over the 49ers, which would prove to be crucial at the end of the season. Both teams finished 10–6, but the Falcons earned a wild card berth by nature of their season sweep.

# Bibliography

**ARTICLES**

Various, in *Daily News, New York Post, New York Times, Sports Illustrated, USA Today*

**BOOKS**

National Football League. *The Official NFL 2002 Record & Fact Book*. New York: Workman, 2002.

___. *The NFL's Official Encyclopedic History of Professional Football*. New York: Macmillan, 1973.

___. *The Super Bowl*. New York: Simon & Schuster, 1990.

Baxter, Russell S., and John Hassan, eds. *ESPN The Ultimate Pro Football Guide*. New York: ESPN Books/Hyperion, 1998.

Brown, Jerry, and Michael Morrison, eds. *2002 ESPN Information Please Sports Almanac*. New York: ESPN Books/ Hyperion, 2002.

Bouchette, Ed. *The Pittsburgh Steelers*. New York: St. Martin's Griffin, 1994.

Eskenazi, Gerald. *Gang Green: An Irreverent Look Behind the Scenes at Thirty-Eight (Well, Thirty-Seven) Seasons of New York Jets Football Futility*. New York: Simon & Schuster, 1998.

Fulks, Matt, ed. *Super Bowl Sunday: The Day America Stops.* Lenexa, Kans.: Addax Publishing Group, 2000.

Green, Tim. *The Dark Side of the Game.* New York: Warner Books, 1996.

Kanner, Bernice. *The Super Bowl of Advertising.* Princeton, N.J.: Bloomberg Press, 2003.

Kramer, Jerry. *Instant Replay.* With Dick Schaap. Cleveland: New American Library, 1968.

Kriegel, Mark. *Namath: A Biography.* New York: Viking, 2004.

Lichtenstein, Michael. *The New York Giants Trivia Book, Revised and Updated.* New York: St. Martin's Griffin, 2001.

MacCambridge, Michael. *America's Game.* New York: Random House, 2004.

MacCambridge, Michael, ed.. *ESPN SportsCentury.* New York: ESPN Books/Hyperion, 1999.

Matuszak, John. *Cruisin' with the Tooz.* With Steve Delson . New York: Charter Books, 1988.

Miller, Jeff. *Going Long.* New York: McGraw Hill, 2003.

Neft, David S., Richard M. Cohen, and Rick Korch. *The Sports Encyclopedia Pro Football, 15th Edition, 1972-1996.* New York: St. Martin's Griffin, 1997.

Payton, Walter. *Never Die Easy.* With Don Yaeger . New York: Villard Books, 2000.

Plimpton, George. *Paper Lion.* New York: Harper & Row, 1966.

Weiss, Don. *The Making of the Super Bowl.* With Chuck Day. Chicago: Contemporary Books, 2003.

Whittingham, Richard. *Rites of Autumn,* New York: Free Press, 2001.

## PRIMARY WEBSITES

espn.com

Internet Movie Database, www.imdb.com.

National Football League, www.nfl.com

NFL Pro Football college draft history, www.drafthistory.com
Super Bowl home page, www.superbowl.com
USA Today Online, www.usatoday.com
www.pro-football-reference.com


**SECONDARY WEBSITES**

Brigham Young University (www.byucougars.com)
Clemson University (www.clemsontigers.com)
Colgate University (athletics.colgate.edu/Football)
Florida State University (www.seminoles.com)
Indiana University (www.iuhoosiers.com)
Kansas State University (www.k-statesports.com)
Louisiana State University (www.lsusports.com)
Michigan State University (www.msuspartans.com)
Mississippi State University (www.mstateathletics.com)
Northwestern University (www.nusports.com)
Oklahoma University (www.soonersports.com)
Oregon State University (www.osubeavers.com)
Purdue University (www.purduesports.com)
Sam Houston State University (www.gobearkats.com)
Texas Christian University (www.gofrogs.com)
United States Military Academy (goarmysports.college
    sports.com)
University of Arkansas (www.hogwired.com)
University of California at Los Angeles (www.uclabruins. com)
University of Georgia (www.georgiadogs.com)
University of Idaho (www.uiathletics.com)
University of Miami (www.hurricanesports.com)
University of Michigan (www.mgoblue.com)
University of Minnesota (www.gophersports.com)
University of Nebraska (www.huskers.com)
University of Texas (www.texassports.com)
West Virginia University (www.msnsportsnet.com)

# Index

# About the Author

Walter Harvey was born in the Bronx and educated at Fordham University. As a youngster, he possessed blazing speed and Largent-like hands, which was often good enough to get him picked second or third in most neighborhood pick-up games. Since abandoning his dream to bring touch football to the Summer Olympics, he has worked primarily in the book publishing industry and is currently a copywriter for an advertising agency. He is the author of *The Super Bowl's Most Wanted*, also available from Potomac Books, Inc. Walter lives in Highland Mills, New York, with his wife, Larissa, and children, Megan and Joseph.